EACH HAPPINESS
RINGED BY LIONS

JANE HIRSHFIELD

Each Happiness Ringed by Lions

SELECTED POEMS

BLOODAXE BOOKS

ISBN: 978 1 85224 693 8

First published 2005 by
Bloodaxe Books Ltd,
Eastburn,
South Park,
Hexham
Northumberland NE46 1BS.

Reprinted 2016, 2019, 2020, 2022

www.bloodaxebooks.com
For further information about Bloodaxe titles
please visit our website and join our mailing list
or write to the above address for a catalogue.

Supported using public funding by
**ARTS COUNCIL
ENGLAND**

Printed in Great Britain by Bell & Bain Limited, Glasgow, Scotland, on
acid-free paper sourced from mills with FSC chain of custody certification.

For Carl

ACKNOWLEDGEMENTS

This first UK edition of Jane Hirshfield's poetry is drawn from her five US collections: *Alaya* (Quarterly Review of Literature, 1982), *Of Gravity & Angels* (Wesleyan University Press, 1988), *The October Palace* (HarperPerennial, 1994), *The Lives of the Heart* (HarperPerennial, 1997) and *Given Sugar, Given Salt* (HarperCollins, 2001).

Epigraph from Yehuda Amichai translated by Yehuda Amichai and Red Hughes. The epigraphs from Dante and Praxilla are in English versions by Jane Hirshfield.

CONTENTS

FROM **The Lives of the Heart** (1994-1997)

I. *Heart Starting and Stopping in the Late Dark*

from

GIVEN SUGAR,
GIVEN SALT

(1997–2001)

The Envoy

One day in that room, a small rat.
Two days later, a snake.

Who, seeing me enter,
whipped the long stripe of his
body under the bed,
then curled like a docile house-pet.

I don't know how either came or left.
Later, the flashlight found nothing.

For a year I watched
as something – terror? happiness? grief? –
entered and then left my body.

Not knowing how it came in,
Not knowing how it went out.

It hung where words could not reach it.
It slept where light could not go.
Its scent was neither snake nor rat,
neither sensualist nor ascetic.

There are openings in our lives
of which we know nothing.

Through them
the belled herds travel at will,
long-legged and thirsty, covered with foreign dust.

Mathematics

I have envied those
who make something
useful, sturdy –
a chair, a pair of boots.

Even a soup,
rich with potatoes and cream.

Or those who fix, perhaps,
a leaking window:
strip out the old cracked putty,
lay down cleanly the line of the new.

You could learn,
the mirror tells me, late at night,
but lacks conviction.
One reflected eyebrow quivers a little.

I look at this
borrowed apartment –
everywhere I question it,
the wallpaper's pattern matches.

Yesterday a woman
showed me
a building shaped
like the overturned hull of a ship,

its roof trusses, under the plaster,
lashed with soaked rawhide,
the columns' marble
painted to seem like wood.
Though possibly it was the other way around?

I look at my unhandy hand,
innocent,
shaped as the hands of others are shaped.
Even the pen it holds is a mystery, really.

Rawhide, it writes,
and *chair*, and *marble*.
Eyebrow.

Later the woman asked me –
I recognised her then,
my sister, my own young self –

Does a poem enlarge the world,
or only our idea of the world?

How do you take one from the other,
I lied, or did not lie,
in answer.

Red Berries

Again the pyrocanthus berries redden in rain,
as if return were return.

It is not.

The familiar is not the thing it reminds of.
Today's *yes* is different from yesterday's *yes*.
Even *no*'s adamance alters.

From painting to painting,
century to century,
the tipped-over copper pot spills out different light;
the cut-open beeves,
their caged and muscled display,
are on one canvas radiant, pure; obscene on another.

In the end it is simple enough –

The woman of this morning's mirror
was a stranger
to the woman of last night's;
the passionate dreams of the one who slept
flit empty and thin
from the one who awakens.

One woman washes her face,
another picks up the boar-bristled hairbrush,
a third steps out of her slippers.
That each will die in the same bed means nothing to them.

Our one breath follows another like spotted horses, no two alike.

Black manes and white manes, they gallop.
Piebald and skewbald, eyes flashing sorrow, they too will pass.

The Room

For two years it lay almost unentered,
almost unoccupied,
except for an insect-hatch of empty cartons.

Then something spiraled,
stirred in a corner, demanded.

And so came the sanding and painting,
the washing of windows,
replacing the cracked half-glass of the door.
So came a bed, a wooden dresser, a desk.

Lain over the dresser's top, a dowry-cloth
from Uzbekistan,
embroidered, cheerful, worn, absurdly expensive.
Before the desk, a chair with woven seat.

The hunt for a rug began.

And during all that time, no idea at all
of why these choices of furniture, this use.
Late, the realisation that something was being courted.

And then a small tremble of exhilaration and fear –

for still it was uncertain what was being prepared for,
when the guest would come or in whose shape,
which half-starved, shivering hopes might follow it in.

Apple

I woke and remembered
nothing of what I was dreaming.

The day grew light, then dark again –
In all its rich hours, what happened?

A few weeds pulled, a few cold flowers
carried inside for the vase.
A little reading. A little tidying and sweeping.

I had vowed to do nothing I did not wish
to do that day, and kept my promise.

Once, a certain hope came close
and then departed. Passed by me in its familiar
shawl, scented with iodine woodsmoke.

I did not speak to it, nor it to me.
Yet still the habit of warmth traveled
between us, like an apple shared by old friends –

One takes a bite, then the other.
They do this until it is gone.

A Hand

A hand is not four fingers and a thumb.

Nor is it palm and knuckles,
not ligaments or the fat's yellow pillow,
not tendons, star of the wristbone, meander of veins.

A hand is not the thick thatch of its lines
with their infinite dramas,
nor what it has written,
not on the page,
not on the ecstatic body.

Nor is the hand its meadows of holding, of shaping –
not sponge of rising yeast-bread,
not rotor pin's smoothness,
not ink.

The maple's green hands do not cup
the proliferant rain.
What empties itself falls into the place that is open.

A hand turned upward holds only a single, transparent question.

Unanswerable, humming like bees, it rises, swarms, departs.

Habit

The shoes put on each time
left first, then right.

The morning potion's teaspoon
of sweetness stirred always
for seven circlings – no fewer, no more –
into the cracked blue cup.

Touching the pocket for wallet,
for keys,
before closing the door.

How did we come
to believe these small rituals' promise,
that we are today the selves we yesterday knew,
tomorrow will be?

How intimate and unthinking,
the way the toothbrush is shaken dry after use,
the part we wash first in the bath.

Which habits we learned from others
and which are ours alone we may never know.
Unbearable to acknowledge
how much they are themselves our fated life.

Open the traveling suitcase –

There the beloved red sweater,
bright tangle of necklace, earrings of amber.
Each confirming: I chose these, I.

But habit is different: it chooses.
And we, its good horse,
opening our mouths at even the sight of the bit.

Rebus

You work with what you are given,
the red clay of grief,
the black clay of stubbornness going on after.
Clay that tastes of care or carelessness,
clay that smells of the bottoms of rivers or dust.

Each thought is a life you have lived or failed to live,
each word is a dish you have eaten or left on the table.
There are honeys so bitter
no one would willingly choose to take them.
The clay takes them: honey of weariness, honey of vanity,
honey of cruelty, fear.

This rebus – slip and stubbornness,
bottom of river, my own consumed life –
when will I learn to read it
plainly, slowly, uncolored by hope or desire?
Not to understand it, only to see.

As water given sugar sweetens, given salt grows salty,
we become our choices.
Each *yes*, each *no* continues,
this one a ladder, that one an anvil or cup.

The ladder leans into its darkness.
The anvil leans into its silence.
The cup sits empty.

How can I enter this question the clay has asked?

Waking This Morning Dreamless After Long Sleep

But with this sentence:
'Use your failures for paper.'
Meaning, I understood,
the backs of failed poems, but also my life.

Whose far side I begin now to enter –

A book imprinted without seeming reason,
each blank day bearing on its reverse, in random order,
the mad-set type of another.
December 12, 1960. April 4, 1981. 13th of August, 1974 –

Certain words bleed through to the unwritten pages.
To call this memory offers no solace.

'Even in sleep, the heavy millstones turning.'

I do not know where the words come from,
what the millstones,
where the turning may lead.

I, a woman forty-five, beginning to gray at the temples,
putting pages of ruined paper
into a basket, pulling them out again.

Poem Holding Its Heart in One Fist

Each pebble in this world keeps
its own counsel.

Certain words – these, for instance –
may be keeping a pronoun hidden.
Perhaps the lover's *you*
or the solipsist's *I*.
Perhaps the philosopher's willowy *it*.

The concealment plainly delights.

Even a desk will gather
its clutch of secret, half-crumpled papers,
eased slowly, over years,
behind the backs of drawers.

Olives adrift in the altering brine-bath
etch onto their innermost pits
a few furrowed salts that will never be found by the tongue.

Yet even with so much withheld,
so much unspoken,
potatoes are cooked with butter and parsley,
and buttons affixed to their sweater.
Invited guests arrive, then dutifully leave.

And this poem, afterward, washes its breasts
with soap and trembling hands, disguising nothing.

Leather

There are times I feel myself cow stripped of her leather.

The hide going on without me,
flensed, vat-dipped, beaten to pliable smoothness.

What remains – awkward, vaguely aware
that something is missing, but what? – continues
its looking outward, evenly breathes.

Sunlight, wind, the black, inquiring noses of others:
sharp now as the knife.

Muscled unjacketed egg.
Impossible butcher's diagram walking. Beginning to graze.

This Was Once a Love Poem

This was once a love poem,
before its haunches thickened, its breath grew short,
before it found itself sitting,
perplexed and a little embarrassed,
on the fender of a parked car,
while many people passed by without turning their heads.

It remembers itself dressing as if for a great engagement.
It remembers choosing these shoes,
this scarf or tie.

Once, it drank beer for breakfast,
drifted its feet
in a river side by side with the feet of another.

Once it pretended shyness, then grew truly shy,
dropping its head so the hair would fall forward,
so the eyes would not be seen.

It spoke with passion of history, of art.
It was lovely then, this poem.
Under its chin, no fold of skin softened.
Behind the knees, no pad of yellow fat.
What it knew in the morning it still believed at nightfall.
An unconjured confidence lifted its eyebrows, its cheeks.

The longing has not diminished.
Still it understands. It is time to consider a cat,
the cultivation of African violets or flowering cactus.

Yes, it decides:
Many miniature cacti, in blue and red painted pots.

When it finds itself disquieted
by the pure and unfamiliar silence of its new life,
it will touch them – one, then another –
with a single finger outstretched like a tiny flame.

Dream Notebook

What will become of these
my many lives,
abandoned each morning abruptly to their own fates?

Of the fox who stopped to look up at me,
bright death stippling her muzzle,
and announced – clearly, simply – 'I was hungry'?
Of the engine left half-disassembled,
the unmendable roof leaks, the waiting packed bags?

Cloudbellies of horses drinking at sunset.
Fierce embraces remembered half a day if at all.

Even the bedside jar of minute and actual seashells
wavers and thins –
though each was lifted, chosen,
I no longer recall whether in joy or distraction,
in foreknowledge or false belief.

How much more elusive, these half-legible scribblings.
If souvenirs at all, they are someone else's.
As each of my memories,
it seems, is destined to be someone else's,

to belong to a woman who
looks faintly like me and whom I wish well,
as one would any stranger passed in a shop, on the street.

Button

It likes both to enter and to leave,
actions it seems to feel as a kind of hide-and-seek.
It knows nothing of what the cloth believes
of its magus-like powers.

If fastening and unfastening are its nature,
it doesn't care about its nature.

It likes the caress of two fingers
against its slightly thickened edges.
It likes the scent and heat of the proximate body.
The exhilaration of the washing is its wild pleasure.

Amoralist, sensualist, dependent of cotton thread,
its sleep is curled like a cat to a patch of sun,
calico and round.

Its understanding is the understanding
of honey and jasmine, of letting what happens come.

A button envies no neighboring button,
no snap, no knot, no polyester-braided toggle.
It rests on its red-checked shirt in serene disregard.

It is its own story, completed.

Brevity and longevity mean nothing to a button carved of horn.

Nor do old dreams of passion disturb it,
though once it wandered the ten thousand grasses
with the musk-fragrance caught in its nostrils;
though once it followed – it did, I tell you – that wind for miles.

Always She Reads the Same Translation

Always she reads the same translation,
and so over decades not one comma alters.

The letters' ascenders and descenders
travel no further
into their yearning toward spirit or body,
nor do they ever pursue that goal with a lessened passion.
The page gutters' margins do not fatten or thin.

Though she has had the poem
long by heart,
she takes the volume from the shelf each time.

Not once has the page grown a single gray hair;
and the title, at first in a foreign language,
remains in a foreign language –
but dear to her now as the furnishings of her own house,
strange only as a chair or table,
looked at sufficiently hard, is strange.

There are those who think the poem says something simple.
There are those who do not see themselves in its ink.

For her the poem –
or in the end, three words of it, just three –
is the gaze of a first lover on the body,
is an arc-welder's cutting torch showering sparks,
is a nightmare.

For these reasons, she keeps returning.
She is looking for something it looks for also, in her.

No lion's sudden tooth tearing the core,
it is the tooth of a rat gnawing.
It eats slowly and she lives, moving a little.

Only When I Am Quiet and Do Not Speak

Only when I am quiet for a long time
and do not speak
do the objects of my life draw near.

Shy, the scissors and spoons, the blue mug.
Hesitant even the towels,
for all their intimate knowledge and scent of fresh bleach.

How steady their regard as they ponder,
dreaming and waking,
the entrancement of my daily wanderings and tasks.
Drunk on the honey of feelings, the honey of purpose,
they seem to be thinking,
a quiet judgment that glistens between the glass doorknobs.

Yet theirs is not the false reserve
of a scarcely concealed ill-will,
nor that other, active shying: of pelted rocks.

No, not that. For I hear the sigh of happiness
each object gives off
if I glimpse for even an instant the actual instant –

As if they believed it possible
I might join
their circle of simple, passionate thusness,
their hidden rituals of luck and solitude,
the joyous gap in them where appears in us the pronoun *I*.

Red Onion, Cherries, Boiling Potatoes, Milk –

Here is a soul, accepting nothing.
Obstinate as a small child
refusing tapioca, peaches, toast.

The cheeks are streaked, but dry.
The mouth is firmly closed in both directions.

Ask, if you like,
if it is merely sulking, or holding out for better.
The soup grows cold in the question.
The ice cream pools in its dish.

Not this, is all it knows. Not this.
As certain cut flowers refuse to drink in the vase.

And the heart, from its great distance, watches, helpless.

Inflection Finally Ungraspable by Grammar

I haven't yet found the pronoun through which to touch it directly.
You may feel differently.
You may think you can simply reach through all the way
 with your hand, like petting the shoulder of an old dog, who, when
she can no longer stand, lies on her bed, watching her kingdom
 arriving and leaving, arriving and leaving, until at last
it only departs.
We want our lives and deaths to be like that – something formal, a kingdom.
 Filled with the sense of the manyness of existence. As the French say
'Vous' to that which cannot yet be made familiar.
They do this less and less these days, it seems.

Linnaean Problem

I have been wondering why there is no name for that part of poetry's music which is not rhythmic. It is simple to say 'meter', 'drumbeat', 'stress' – but what is the other half called? Prosody, 'sound', melopoeia – each covers both. Rhyme is merely a fraction; assonance, consonance, tune mean only themselves. Perhaps it is like the problem of horse and rider: Easy to have a horse with no rider, impossible to have a rider without, grazing somewhere nearby, a horse. Time exists without the scented, muscular body traveling through it, but no planet, parrot tick, leopard lives free of time. Even the purest singing signals a maculate conception, within an imagination schooled by passage. And so that part of poetry's music made by the untempered mouth, breath, and throat remains, without the measuring hoofbeat, uncapturable silence. A mockingbird's song heard in a mirror; the shadow a dog's night-barking leaves on the dark.

All Evening, Each Time I Started to Say It

All evening, each time I started to say it,
something would interrupt.
It was not a thought so very large –
it could in fact have slipped through any window
cracked open a bit for air.
Yet each time I started to say it, at that table,
someone else would speak, the moment would pass.
After the fifth time this happened, I began to be amused.
Runt-of-the-litter thought, I thought, *unable to get to the tit*.
Then suddenly wanted to lift it up,
to feed it an eyedropper's measure of mare's milk,
some warmed sugar water, a little colostrum of badger.
It suddenly seemed to me the kind of thought,
not large, on which a life might turn.
There are many such: unheard, unspoken.
Their blind eyes open and close,
the almost audible valves of their hearts.
But all evening, each time I started to say it,
something would interrupt, the moment would pass.

In Praise of Coldness

'If you wish to move your reader,'
Chekhov wrote, 'you must write more coldly.'

Herakleitos recommended, 'A dry soul is best.'

And so at the center of many great works
is found a preserving dispassion,
like the vanishing point of quattrocento perspective,
or the tiny packets of desiccant enclosed
in a box of new shoes or seeds.

But still the vanishing point
is not the painting,
the silica is not the blossoming plant.

Chekhov, dying, read the timetables of trains.
To what more earthly thing could he have been faithful? –
Scent of rocking distances,
smoke of blue trees out the window,
hampers of bread, pickled cabbage, boiled meat.

Scent of the knowable journey.

Neither a person entirely broken
nor one entirely whole can speak.

In sorrow, pretend to be fearless. In happiness, tremble.

A Cedary Fragrance

Even now,
decades after,
I wash my face with cold water –

Not for discipline,
nor memory,
nor the icy, awakening slap,

but to practise
choosing
to make the unwanted wanted.

The Lie

Like a moveable theme drawn into being by a great composer,
 who places it into one part of the music, then another,

sometimes folding or inverting it like shirting-fabric,
sometimes setting it upside down like a stone or a swarm of bees
 that knows neither top nor bottom,
 yet by balance remains recognisable and whole,
the old lie comes.

Its notes like white-faced cows looking back in strong starlight.

Difficult to say why this so pleases.
Perhaps it is not the outcome, but the listening,
 the being asked once more to listen.

Happiness Is Harder

To read a book of poetry
from back to front,
there is the cure for certain kinds of sadness.

A person has only to choose.
What doesn't matter; just *that* –

This coffee. That dress.
'Here is the time I would like to arrive.'
'Today, I will wash the windows.'

Happiness is harder.

Consider the masters' description
of awakened existence, how seemingly simple:
Hungry, I eat; sleepy, I sleep.
Is this choosing completely, or not at all?

In either case, everything seems to conspire against it.

The Gallop

There are days the whole house moves at a gallop.
Bookshelves and counters, bottles of aspirin and oil,
chairs, saucepans, and towels.

I can barely encircle the neck
of a bounding pen with my fingers
before it breaks free of their notions;
open the door before the dog
of lop-eared hopes leaps through it;
pick up the paper before it goes up as kindling.

Barely eat before something snatches
the toast from my plate,
drains the last mouthfuls of coffee out of my cup.

Even these words –
before the blue ink-track has dried on the paper,
they've already been read
and agreed to or flung aside for others I don't yet know of,

and well before
I have dressed or brushed out the braid of my hair,
a woman with my own shadow
has showered and chosen her earrings, bought groceries
and fallen in love, grown tired, grown old.

Her braid in the mirror shines with new ribbons of silver,
like the mane of a heavy warhorse.
He stands in the silence as if after battle, sides heaving, spent.

Pillow

Some pillows are made of down, feathers,
and striped cotton ticking,
some of wool or dried herb flowers,
others of thought.

The thought of a good sandwich
in the lunch bag, for instance –
provolone slices and garden tomato,
a little Dijon and mayonnaise – can be a pillow,

comforting as the memory of being,
for one moment,
not entirely embarrassed to be human.

Able, say, to meet the gaze
of a cow or a horse with eyes neither arrogant
nor lowered, to offer a carrot
not as propitiation or bribe but simple friendship.

Friendship can be simple,
like the pillow of a horseshoe's lucky curve
above a door where it's needed.

'Here,' I said to my friend when he was dying.
'Here,' he replied.

There was nothing more to ask of one another,
though we spoke a while longer,
words like river pebbles, some black, some white,
wrapped in a handkerchief's tied-together purse.

I could not eat them,
so I put them under my pillow that night,
and slept well,
without dismay or turning,
though he would continue dying, though I would live.

His look, those days: plain as water, undeterred
by the ongoing disassemblage.
A little greedy, but also ready, prepared.

Whatever came, he told me, would be his own luck.

We held hands a time,
then together let go that touch,
together turned to our separate tasks,

like the two hands
of a person arranging the blankets and pillow
just so before sleeping,
settling the one day in order to enter the next.

'Nothing Lasts'

'Nothing lasts' –
how bitterly the thought attends each loss.

'Nothing lasts' –
a promise also of consolation.

Grief and hope
the skipping rope's two ends,
twin daughters of impatience.

One wears a dress of wool, the other cotton.

Great Powers Once Raged Through Your Body

Great powers once raged
through your body, waking and sleeping.
What remains?

A few words, your own or others'.
A freshened affection for silence and rest;
but also for lightning and wind,
familiar to you now as your own coat or shoes.

They lie on the closet floor
in the scent of paint and pinewood,
as if you had picked them out for yourself,
as if you had carried them home.

'What could have happened, has happened.'
The sentence repeating itself in your ear
as a pear repeats itself, each time a little altered,
on every branch of the tree.

Chair, table, dishcloth, bowl –
each thing under your hand or your eyes
you regard now as ally, as friend.

And yet this hard-won composure
feels already a little simple, a little meek –
like a painting
of yellow houses or fields, before
the narrow slashes of red have been riveted in.

'A Carbon-based Life Form'

A person tired from happiness grows sober.

Another, worn through
by sadness, stumbles into a kind of joy.

It is like a dog alone in a house, barking to hear its own kind.

Nothing needs to be added. Yet we do.

Minotaur

Once a minotaur,
a secret revealed becomes a rock,
a tree, a cow like any other.
Only the one who once held it, seeing it
thus diminished, strokes the rough bark or small ears,
leans against the silent, cold surface with sorrow,
remembers it in its former, fearsome glory.

Ladder

A man tips back his chair, all evening.

Years later, the ladder of small indentations
still marks the floor. Walking across it, then stopping.

Rarely are what is spoken and what is meant the same.

Mostly the mouth says one thing, the thighs and knees
say another, the floor hears a third.

Yet within us,
objects and longings are not different.
They twist on the stem of the heart, like ripening grapes.

Blue Window

In the dream, some believe, everything matters equally.

The protagonist who sits at the table
no more or less the dreamer's necessity than the table
or the small spoon she finds at rest in her left hand.

The clink of soup spoon stirred against soup bowl
no more nourishing or less nourishing than the red soup.
In the dream, the ears drink and drink –
how thirsty they must have been for that sound.

The legs of the table drink too, like lapping panthers,
four of them gathered companionably
around the legs of the woman holding the spoon,
as if a sudden, pure democracy, or a painter's peaceable kingdom.

As if the chorus reentering after the aria's close,
or a blue window opening out of a pale orange wall.

As if a durable assuaging.

As if the cell in the breast and not the breast,
or if the breast then that alone and not the woman,

though all things in the dream be equal,
not the woman,
neither the one who eats and listens

nor she mercifully, these minutes longer, dreaming.

Muslin

'I never knew when he would come,'
my friend said of her lover,
'though often it was late in the afternoon.'

Behind her back the first plum blossoms
had started to open,
few as the stars that salt the earliest dusk.

'Finally weeks would go by, then months,'
she added, 'but always I let him in.
It made me strong, you see,

'the gradual going without him.
I think it taught me a kind of surrender,
though of course I hated it too.'

Why he would appear or stay away
she never fathomed –
'I couldn't ask. And that also seemed only good.'

A small bird fluttered silent behind her left shoulder,
then settled on some hidden branch.
'Do you ask the weather why it comes or goes?'

She was lovely, my friend, even the gray
of her hair was lovely. A listening rope-twist
half pity, half envy tightened its length in my chest.

'When he came, you see, I could trust
that was what he wanted.
What I wanted never mattered at all.'

The hands on her lap seemed quiet,
even contented.
I noticed something unspoken begin to

billow and shimmer between us,
weightless as muslin,
but neither of us moved to lift it away.

Walker Evans Interior, 1936

From the photograph it's impossible to tell
whether one of the chair legs is short
or the floorboards sag.

But you can feel how every time
the woman comes in from the weather
and sits by the food safe
to unlace her cold boots and the day's mud-stiffness

she knows the sudden tock of shifting balance.
How the whole interior shudders and settles again.

I feel it now, traveling
through my own ease of thigh and light knock of seatbone
and into the simple good luck of my ribs.

The bump of a kind of hope against its lock,
or a hard kiss against her,
the kind you'd only miss after it stopped.

Like an Ant Carrying Her Bits of Leaf or Sand

Like an ant carrying her bits of leaf or sand,
the poem carries its words.
Moving one, then another, into place.

Something in an ant is sure where these morsels belong,
but the ant could not explain this.
Something in a poem is certain where its words belong,
but the poet could not explain this.

All day the ant obeys an inexplicable order.
All day the poet obeys an incomprehensible demand.

The world changes or does not change by these labors;
the geode peeled open gives off its cold scent or does not.
But that is no concern of the ant's, of the poem's.

The work of existence devours its own unfolding.
What dissolves will dissolve –
you, reader, and I, and all our quick angers and longings.
The potato's sugary hunger for growing larger.
The unblinking heat of the tiger.

No thimble of cloud or stone that will not vanish,
and still the rearrangements continue.

The ant's work belongs to the ant.
The poem carries love and terror, or it carries nothing.

Self-portrait in a Borrowed Cabin

One night eating potatoes pan-fried,
the next night baked, two nights later, mashed.
A hummingbird drives at the evening fuchsia,
still sunlit this far north.
Because I have seen this before, I think:
My hummingbird is drinking. And later, *my four-point buck* –
who also likes the red flowers.
If the hummingbird is thinking, *my pendant fuchsia,
my watching human,* I will not know it.
Then in broad evening brightness the raccoon
races its shadow across the mown grass.
Not *my raccoon* – it's Eleanor and Richard's, next door.
Each of us racing with him, making our own
for a little while, as travelers do, what is no one's.
Every third morning here I wake from another nightmare,
and still I find myself thinking: *paradise, bliss.*

The Contract

The woman who gave me the rosebush
reminds me:
'Cut it back hard.'

The stems resist.

Thorns and weedy twig-thickets
catch on jacket sleeve, on gloves.
Core-wood splinters green under the shears.

Impossible to believe
that so little left will lead to fragrance.

Still, my hands move quickly,
adding their signature branch by branch,
agreeing to loss.

Poem with Two Endings

Say 'death' and the whole room freezes –
even the couches stop moving,
even the lamps.
Like a squirrel suddenly aware it is being looked at.

Say the word continuously,
and things begin to go forward.
Your life takes on
the jerky texture of an old film strip.

Continue saying it,
hold it moment after moment inside the mouth,
it becomes another syllable.
A shopping mall swirls around the corpse of a beetle.

Death is voracious, it swallows all the living.
Life is voracious, it swallows all the dead.
Neither is ever satisfied, neither is ever filled,
each swallows and swallows the world.

The grip of life is as strong as the grip of death.

(but the vanished, the vanished beloved, o where?)

A Scale Weighs the Outer World
in Pounds and Ounces

A winch,
with its drag drum and hoist drum, is strong.

Grief is stronger,
yet weighs no more than the pattern
of leaf and sun on the bark of a tree.

Joy, too, is strong,
yet changes no more than the cloth of a curtain
pulled open rather than closed.

Emotion – handless and eyeless –
runs through the body like current through copper wire.
Equally innocent of its ends, equally voracious.

A scale weighs the outer world in pounds and ounces.
The sum does not alter,
whatever happens within and between us.

One will feel this as blessing, another as horror.

Bone

The living dog
has found the old dog's toy.
She brings it to the kitchen,
the blue rubber a little cracked
from all that time outside.
My memories,
my counting and expectations,
mean nothing to her;
my sadness, though,
does puzzle her a moment.
Then she keeps on chewing.
Time's instruments are thumb piano,
oboe, ocarina, flute, and dog.
Its movements
run through her body flawlessly.
Only we sing with a catch in the throat.
She hears the thought. – 'Catch?'
She's ready.

Moment

A person wakes from sleep
and does not know for a time
who she is, who he is.

This happens in a lifetime
once or twice.
It has happened to you, no doubt.

Some in that moment
panic,
some sigh with pleasure.

How each kind later envies the other,
who must so love their lives.

Elephant Seals, Año Nuevo Preserve

They remind of the walnut's almost welded-in sweetness.
They remind of the unbribable cat.
They remind of the roof, its sloped unconcern for above or below.

Individual and silent, each thick-glassed bottle.
Clarified and complete-in-itself, each shoulder-hunched stone.

Consider an engine, enclosed in its alien hums and whistles.
Consider a two-ton beetle, clacking its varnished sheen.

Like an onion growing larger without any limit:
ungraspable, its umbilical sugars and heat,
its inner moistness wrapped in the thinnest of papers.
Three layers, four at most define it –
on one side rampantly onion, on the other impassive soil.

So it is with these groundfallen rainclouds,
these past ripe, prize-winning melons out-buckling their skin.

Though here, where one being ends, an equal begins.
Sometimes lying side by side like companionable rowboats,
sometimes touching with sensitive noses –
quick as hollow-boned plovers then, light as sand flies.

In every unknowable earth-fold, unknowable ardor.

Rock

What appears to be stubbornness,
refusal, or interruption,
is to it a simple privacy. It broods
its one thought like a quail her clutch of eggs.

Mosses and lichens
listen outside the locked door.
Stars turn the length of one winter, then the next.

Rocks fill their own shadows without hesitation,
and do not question silence,
however long.
Nor are they discomforted by cold, by rain, by heat.

The work of a rock is to ponder whatever is:
an act that looks singly like prayer,
but is not prayer.

As for this boulder,
its meditations are slow but complete.

Someday, its thinking worn out, it will be
carried away by an ant.
A *Mystrium camillae*,
perhaps, caught in some equally diligent,
equally single pursuit of a thought of her own.

One Life Is Spent, the Other Spends Us

One life is spent, the other spends us.

Rarely, they touch –
like a cat for the first time meeting itself in a mirror.

In the world, mirrors are few.
The slightest wind dissolves them.

In a life, the moments of recognition are few.

Consciousness does not hate or love, it neither grieves nor longs.
Walking and breathing are not its nature.
It is.

Yet something passes and ends, grows wet in rain then dries,

and the small bowl of kibble empties into a delicate, spotted paw,
a tail slightly kinked, a preference for one windowsill
over another.

August Day

You work with what you are given –
today I am blessed, today I am given luck.

It takes the shape of a dozen ripening fruit trees,
a curtain of pole beans, a thicket of berries.
It takes the shape of a dozen empty hours.

In them is neither love nor love's muster of losses,
in them is no chance for harm or for good.
Does even my humanness matter?
A bear would be equally happy, this August day,
fat on the simple sweetness plucked between thorns.

There are some who may think, 'How pitiful, how lonely.'
Others must murmur, 'How lazy.'

I agree with them all: pitiful, lonely, lazy.
Lost to the earth and to heaven,
thoroughly drunk on its whiskeys, I wander my kingdom.

Balance

Balance is noticed most when almost failed of –

in an elephant's delicate wavering
on her circus stool, for instance,
or that moment
when a ladder starts to tip but steadies back.

There are, too, its mysterious departures.

Hours after the dishes are washed and stacked,
a metal bowl clangs to the floor,
the weight of drying water all that altered;
a painting vertical for years
one morning – *why?* – requires a restoring tap.

You have felt it disappearing
from your own capricious heart –
a restlessness enters, the smallest leaning begins.

Already then inevitable,
the full collision,
the life you will describe afterward always as 'after'.

Identity

Decades after a man leaves the Church,
still he is called the priest.

Many years since she set down her bow,
a woman remains the cellist.

The one who seduced so many is content
now to sip her tea,
and still she is looked at with envy and hatred.

The one who held life and death
in his mouth
no longer speaks at all, yet still he is feared.

The unmoving dancer rehearses her steps.
Again, perfection eludes her.

Fate loosens its grip. The bruises stay.

For Horses, Horseflies

We know nothing of the lives of others.
Under the surface, what strange desires,
what rages, weaknesses, fears.

Sometimes it breaks into the daily paper
and we shake our heads in wonder –
'Who would behave in such a way?' we ask.

Unspoken the thought, 'Let me not be tested.'
Unspoken the thought, 'Let me not be known.'

Under the surface, something that whispers,
'Anything can be done.'

For horses, horseflies. For humans, shame.

Speed and Perfection

How quickly the season of apricots is over –
a single night's wind is enough.
I kneel on the ground, lifting one, then the next.
Eating those I can, before the bruises appear.

Optimism

More and more I have come to admire resilience.
Not the simple resistance of a pillow, whose foam
returns over and over to the same shape, but the sinuous
tenacity of a tree: finding the light newly blocked on one side,
it turns in another. A blind intelligence, true.
But out of such persistence arose turtles, rivers,
mitochondria, figs – all this resinous, unretractable earth.

Five-legged Chair

Hunger, fear, curiosity, desire –
these four
would have more than sufficed.

By what sudden lurch
of kindness
or small moment's inattention
were creation's fierce gods possessed,

to give us this supernumerary joy?

Tree

It is foolish
to let a young redwood
grow next to a house.

Even in this
one lifetime,
you will have to choose.

That great calm being,
this clutter of soup pots and books –

Already the first branch-tips brush at the window.
Softly, calmly, immensity taps at your life.

Silk Cord

In the dream the string had broken
and I was trying to
pick out its beads among all others.

The large coral beads,
the beads of turquoise and ivory –
these were not mine.
Carved and ridged with color, burnished, weighty –
my hands passed over them without regret or pause.

The tiny ones,
of glass,
almost invisible against the white cotton bedspread –
these were mine.

The hole in the center
scarcely discernible as different from the bead itself,
the bead around it
scarcely discernible as different from the bed or floor or air –

with trembling fingers
I lifted them
into the jar my other hand cupped closely to one breast.

Not precious, merely glass, almost invisible.
How terrified I was at the thought of missing even one.

While I live, I thought, *they are mine to care for.*

Then wakened heavy with what I recognised at once
as an entirely warranted grief,

frantic for something plain and clear
and almost without substance,
that I myself had scattered, that I myself must find.

The Silence

One acquaintance says of another,
'I think he's a happy man,'
then pauses.

I see on his face what I also
am thinking,
and wonder what he is remembering,
inside our silence.

I am remembering a funeral,
friend after friend rising to speak
of the lost one.
I did not know him well,
yet still, by one thing he had told me,
wore fully our closeness.

Or perhaps it was even simpler –
to whom else could he say the truth?

I wondered, even then,
how many others attending knew also one thing.
Each secret separate, different,
leading its life now without him:
carrying laundry, washing the windows, straightening up.

As they do, perhaps, I would like to sit down now and rest.

I would like to ponder the flavor
of how much I know of others, how much I do not;
of what of me is known and what is not.

A conversation is overheard on a train, on an airplane,
and even Love cannot know the whole.
It sits in the row behind,
listening quietly to what it is able.
Then the green and red wing-lights blink out;
the train rounds the track's curve and is lost.

Love, also disappearing,
would like to tap the two murmuring ones on the shoulder.
Love would like to say to them,
'Speak more fearlessly – This is the only – Say what you can.'

Politeness forbids it.

Love sits in the row behind,
and quietly listens.
Love lowers its stricken face so no one will see.

Sleep

Horses, yes.
Dogs, old ones especially.
People of course.
Even trees.

Planets, atoms do not.
A bacterium, a virus?
Unlikely.

Pens sleep
most of the time,
but awaken quickly –
one shake
or a few dry strokes suffice.

A fire sleeps by dark,
a cat by daylight,
each curled in a warming circle.
A rock lies still or tumbles,
but cannot sleep.

Does the wool
sleep along with its sheep?
The hoof with its cow?

The finger sleeps
and the ring does not –
what of the vow?

A woman touched by a man
pretends, sometimes,
to sleep,
for the pleasure of letting him think
that she awakens.

After, her thighs
sleep differently from before.

Sometimes the heart
goes sleepless or sleeps for years;
sometimes the mind.

I have tried to talk
with my sleep,
to ask it politely for this or that,
but it only averts its gaze.

'Go away,' it says,
and, 'Leave me alone.'
As if without me
it could be anything at all.

Still, it knows who is slave,
who master.

And so I lavish on it
goosedown and soft cotton,
offer it sweetened milk
or wine,
tuck it into warm blankets
under a window opened just an inch.

Some speak
of entering sleep,
but it is sleep that enters us,
as a farmer, familiar,
confident, enters his field.

Night after night it tills and waters,
so that at times we awaken
buoyant,
other times in inexplicable grief.

And though the child
who refuses to sleep
is right perhaps to be inconsolable –
begging more time,
clutching her bear to her cheek –
she too will finally agree.

Joining the silent magpies
and tough-skinned conch and saguaro;
the swaying mule deer,
suspended pipefish,
and deep-sighing maple –

all who, drifting,
distal,
quilt the drowsy night-song of the mortal.

Clock

There is no substance
that does not carry one inside it,
hands spinning
as the Fates were said to do.

Or, more truly, carry many:
in one body the clock of the knee
and the ankle-clock keep different times,
the swaying metronome of the breast ignores
the solstice curve of rib that supports it.

Nor does the body's clock
govern its soul's,
which may move more quickly or slower –
a divergence seen in some moods
as tragic, comic in others.

All clocks in themselves are serene.
It is their task to run down.

And so the clock of the tree
welcomes its beetles and lichens,
the clock of the house feasts with its termites.

And still the clock of the marrow
spills out its cells gone wrong
and the clock of the family falters, unoiled and forgotten.
The living clock of fallible springs runs
side by side with the death-clock of quartz,
and neither clock can touch the hands of the other.

Some clocks are indifferent and perfect,
others bend over as walking animals under strong wind.

Even the clock of blue, uprisen granite
carries within it
the cooling clock of its own erosion to gruss.

Whole ranges this way disappear, obeying their clocks,
while the clock of a grove of aspen,
in theory immortal,
still shivers each season's gold-leaf into the wind.

A wet dog comes into the kitchen to shake off her wetness.
The drops fall, then dry: a clock's ticking gone suddenly still.

The clock of a memory
not remembered is not stopped,
as the clock of a memory remembered is not stopped.

Neither do these clocks grow larger or smaller,
greater or lesser, more bitter or sweet.
They stay on their walls, their dashboards, their wrists.
There, they are called watches, as if observers,
as if that close to the body they could look back.

Clock of the bamboo dipper that fills with water
then clacks itself empty, unlistened to, year after year;
gravity egg-clock of turned-over three-minute sand;
clock of the isotope's half-life, of a spotted mare come into heat;
star-clocks of Stonehenge, of Chichén Itzá,
of the rotating earth-face that holds two numbers only, light and
 then dark.
Clock of a pickup's engine leaking its oil,
'Three weeks before she needs some, steady as clockwork.'

They do not look back.
They do not look, concerned with neither our terrors nor joys.
Only the eye looks at them,
looks and looks while swimming its river of lubricant tears –
some shuddered in unconcealed loudness;
some whispered silent over the cheekbones and down the chin's
 crevice;
most – steady slipstream of life still living – held for all time.

The merest glimmer, blinked back almost unnoticed,
as the blinking of a watchface goes almost unnoticed, until it is gone.

Ink

Like all liquids,
it is sister to chaos and time:
wanting always
to lose itself in another,
visible only when held in embrace.

It is also like the aurochs
of ancient Europe,
reentering the world with reluctance –
at the threshold, marks of the scoring horns,
their curls, tip-blots, and scratchings.

Some of its substances:

Carbon of lampblack.
Lapis well-powdered.
Rust flakes milled fine.

Certain inks grip their surface,
others soak in.
Still others, like potters' glazes,
require baking –
the paper arrives warm then with its words,
a fresh bread seeded with poppies.

The tulip magnolia
writes first in white ink, then in green.
Each new twig blossoms as ink to the reading mind.

As with the squid's dark cloud
or the writings on certain moth-wings,
some inks are meant to disguise –
the eye of the hawk stares fiercely,
but where is the hawk?

Some glossy, brilliant, expounding,
others darkly impenetrable as sleep,
all consist of pigment, binder, and carrier.

Each part must be compatible with the others.
And so the glueing binder –
shellac, gum arabic, plastic, or resin –
must enter seamlessly
into the carrier's solvent.
In this, ink is like a metaphor well-made.

And like metaphor,
good ink has also its fragrance:
some smell of earth,
others are heady with spirits.

In itself ink is carrier, solvent,
and pigment to thought:
thought, entering ink,
equally transports, rushes, and stays.

Alcohol-based, oil-based, or water,
all inks must eventually dry,
releasing their words from the verb tense
of present-resilient to that of perfected past.

They settle weightless, meaningful as dust.

Until the reader –
an aromatic organic carrier
not unlike any other,
not unlike, say, fresh turpentine meeting old varnish –
redissolves them,
adds back the moistened eye, the moistened mind.

Then the drying and non-drying oils –
petroleum, soya –
unfasten their chemical binding.
The script-melisma unscrolls in the listening ear.

And again the impossible
happens with such ease it is almost unnoticed:

A radish once dipped
in salt and eaten is eaten once more.
A mountain walks in and out of its quantum of fog.
A woman of ancient China paints on her eyebrows.

Then each grain of that salt
passes again through the world-gate,
returned to the black gates of ink, which silently close.

Metempsychosis

Some stories last many centuries,
others only a moment.
All alter over that lifetime like beach-glass,
grow distant and more beautiful with salt.

Yet even today, to look at a tree
and ask the story *Who are you?* is to be transformed.

There is a stage in us where each being, each thing, is a mirror.

Then the bees of self pour from the hive-door,
ravenous to enter the sweetness of flowering nettles and thistle.

Next comes the ringing a stone or violin or empty bucket
gives off –
the immeasurable's continuous singing,
before it goes back into story and feeling.

In Borneo, there are palm trees that walk on their high roots.
Slowly, with effort, they lift one leg then another.

I would like to join that stilted transmigration,
to feel my own skin vertical as theirs:
an ant road, a highway for beetles.

I would like not minding, whatever travels my heart.
To follow it all the way into leaf-form, bark-furl, root-touch,
and then keep walking, unimaginably further.

from

THE LIVES
OF THE HEART

(1994–1997)

The Lives of the Heart

Are ligneous, muscular, chemical.
Wear birch-colored feathers,
green tunnels of horse-tail reed.
Wear calcified spirals, Fibonnacian spheres.
Are edible; are glassy; are clay; blue schist.
Can be burned as tallow, as coal,
can be skinned for garnets, for shoes.
Cast shadows or light;
shuffle; snort; cry out in passion.
Are salt, are bitter,
tear sweet grass with their teeth.
Step silently into blue needle-fall at dawn.
Thrash in the net until hit.
Rise up as cities, as serpentined magma, as maples,
hiss lava-red into the sea.
Leave the strange kiss of their bodies
in Burgess Shale. Can be found, can be lost,
can be carried, broken, sung.
Lie dormant until they are opened by ice,
by drought. Go blind in the service of lace.
Are starving, are sated, indifferent, curious, mad.
Are stamped out in plastic, in tin.
Are stubborn, are careful, are slipshod,
are strung on the blue backs of flies
on the black backs of cows.
Wander the vacant whale-roads, the white thickets
heavy with slaughter.
Wander the fragrant carpets of alpine flowers.
Not one is not held in the arms of the rest, to blossom.
Not one is not given to ecstasy's lions.
Not one does not grieve.
Each of them opens and closes, closes and opens
the heavy gate – violent, serene, consenting, suffering it all.

I.

HEART STARTING AND STOPPING
IN THE LATE DARK

The Heart's Counting Knows Only One

In Sung China,
two monks friends for sixty years
watched the geese pass.
Where are they going?
one tested the other, who couldn't say.

That moment's silence continues.

No one will study their friendship
in the *koan*-books of insight.
No one will remember their names.

I think of them sometimes,
standing, perplexed by sadness,
goose-down sewn into their quilted autumn robes.

Almost swallowed by the vastness of the mountains,
but not yet.

As the barely audible
geese are not yet swallowed;
as even we, my love, will not entirely be lost.

Not Moving Even One Step

The rain falling too lightly to shape
an audible house, an audible tree,
blind, soaking, the old horse waits in his pasture.

He knows the field for exactly what it is:
his limitless mare, his beloved.
Even the mallards sleep in her red body maned
in thistles, hooved in the new green shallows of spring.

Slow rain streams from fetlocks, hips, the lowered head,
while she stands in the place beside him that no one sees.

The muzzles almost touch.
How silently the heart pivots on its hinge.

Secretive Heart

– What's this? This is an old toolshed.
– No, this is a great past love.
YEHUDA AMICHAI

Heart falters, stops
before a Chinese cauldron
still good for boiling water.

It is one of a dozen or more,
it is merely iron,
it is merely old,
there is much else to see.

The few raised marks
on its belly
are useful to almost no one.

Heart looks at it a long time.
What do you see? I ask again,
but it does not answer.

The New Silence

There are times
when the heart closes down,
the metal grate drawn
and padlocked,
the owner's footprints covered by snow.

Someone may come to peer through the glass,
but soon leaves.
Someone may come to clean, but turns away.

What is still inside
settles down for the darkness: clocks stop,
newspapers pass out of date.

The new silence goes unheard
under so many grindings of engines,
so many sounds of construction.

Only the three pigeons,
refusing to eat,
lower their heads and grieve.

Mule Heart

On the days when the rest
have failed you,
let this much be yours –
flies, dust, an unnameable odor,
the two waiting baskets:
one for the lemons and passion,
the other for all you have lost.
Both empty,
it will come to your shoulder,
breathe slowly against your bare arm.
If you offer it hay, it will eat.
Offered nothing,
it will stand as long as you ask.
The little bells of the bridle will hang
beside you quietly,
in the heat and the tree's thin shade.
Do not let its sparse mane deceive you,
or the way the left ear swivels into dream.
This too is a gift of the gods,
calm and complete.

The World Loved by Moonlight

You must try,
the voice said, to become colder.
I understood at once.
It is like the bodies of gods: cast in bronze,
braced in stone. Only something heartless
could bear the full weight.

Salt Heart

I was tired,
half sleeping in the sun.
A single bee
delved the lavender nearby,
and beyond the fence,
a trowel's shoulder knocked a white stone.
Soon, the ringing stopped.
And from somewhere,
a quiet voice said the one word.
Surely a command,
though it seemed more a question,
a wondering perhaps – 'What about joy?'
So long it had been forgotten,
even the thought raised surprise.
But however briefly, there,
in the untuned devotions of bee
and the lavender fragrance,
the murmur of better and worse was unimportant.
From next door, the sound of raking,
and neither courage nor cowardice mattered.
Failure – uncountable failure – did not matter.
Soon enough that gate swung closed,
the world turned back to heart-salt
of wanting, heart-salts of will and grief.
My friend would continue dying, at last
only exhausted, even his wrists thinned with pain.
The river Suffering would take what it
wished of him, then go. And I would stay
and drink on, as the living do, until the rest
would enter into that water – the lavender swept in,
the bee, the swallowed labors of my neighbor.
The ordinary moment swept in, whatever it drowsily holds.
I begin to believe the only sin is distance, refusal.
All others stemming from this. Then come.
Rivers, come. Irrevocable futures, come. Come even joy.
Even now, even here, and though it vanish like him.

On the Beach

Uncountable tiny pebbles
of many colors.

Broken seashells mixed in with whole ones.

Sand dollars, shattered and whole,
the half-gone wing of a gull.

Changed glass
that is like the heart after much pain.
The empty shell of a crab.

A child moves alone in the grey
that is half fog, half wind-blown ocean.

She lifts one pebble, another,
into her pocket.
From time to time takes them out again and looks.

These few and only these. How many? Why?

The waves continue their work of breaking
then rounding the edges.

I would speak to her if I could,
but across the distance what would she hear?
Ocean and ocean. Cry of a fish.

Walk slowly now, small soul, by the edge
of the water. Choose carefully
all you are going to lose, though any of it would do.

Abundant Heart

Because the pelicans circle and dive, the fish

Because the cows are fat, the rains

Because the tree is heavy with pears, the earth

Because the woman grows thin, the heart

Heart Starting and Stopping in the Late Dark

I cannot tell
if this night singing comes
from inside or outside the house,
though today a cricket walked
across my papers on the floor.
He made a little clicking sound
as he passed, from his strange knees,
or his feet on the paper.
He seemed to know where he wanted to get to.
When the dying Bonnard had his nephew add
the new yellow-gold to 'Almond in Blossom',
it was his signature he cancelled for that other.
This late typing, starting and stopping,
is not so different from a cricket's walking
to the night's ear, I think,
if the night had an ear. Perhaps that is what
started him singing wherever he is,
startled by my insomnia into his one word,
which is filled I think with dignity,
which is filled I think with trust.
I would like to go, as at last Bonnard did,
all the way into the world of the living.
To sit there a while in the petals, altering nothing.

Standing Deer

As the house of a person
in age sometimes grows cluttered
with what is
too loved or too heavy to part with,
the heart may grow cluttered.
And still the house will be emptied,
and still the heart.

As the thoughts of a person
in age sometimes grow sparer,
like a great cleanness come into a room,
the soul may grow sparer;
one sparrow song carves it completely.
And still the room is full,
and still the heart.

Empty and filled,
like the curling half-light of morning,
in which everything is still possible and so why not.

Filled and empty,
like the curling half-light of evening,
in which everything now is finished and so why not.

Beloved, what can be, what was,
will be taken from us.
I have disappointed.
I am sorry. I knew no better.

A root seeks water.
Tenderness only breaks open the earth.
This morning, out the window,
three deer stood like a blessing, then vanished.

Da Capo

Take the used-up heart like a pebble
and throw it far out.

Soon there is nothing left.
Soon the last ripple exhausts itself
in the weeds.

Returning home, slice carrots, onions, celery.
Glaze them in oil before adding
the lentils, water, and herbs.

Then the roasted chestnuts, a little pepper, the salt.
Finish with goat cheese and parsley. Eat.
You may do this, I tell you, it is permitted.
Begin again the story of your life.

The Adamantine Perfection of Desire

Nothing more strong
than to be helpless before desire.

No reason,
the simplified heart whispers,
the argument over,
only This.

No longer choosing anything but assent.

Its bowl scraped clean to the bottom,
the skull-bone cup no longer horrifies,
but, rimmed-in-silver, shines.

A spotted dog follows a bitch in heat.
Grey geese fly past us, crying.
The living cannot help but love the world.

Irreversible Heart

Take away
the bird, its hidden singing.
Take away the love.

One branch of maple
flares against
the cedar darkness,

grief that was
always present,
disguised beneath the green.

Take away the small blue table,
the wild apples,
the journey's long perfections.
Bow to the ground.
Walk into the lion day.

Heart Pressing Further

Mustard greens
and a little garlic sautéed in oil,
a few seeds of chili,
pasta added after and tossed.
Outside the steamed windows,
the sound of rain,
and within it a raccoon's walking,
every hair of his body tipped with cold silver.
The ones who are sitting now
know nothing of what he desires in the dark;
they say a few words, continue to eat.
He pauses, lowers his head to
a stone and some leaves.
Night deepens, the rain falls harder.
He lifts his head and goes on.

II.

NOT-YET

Not-Yet

Morning of buttered toast;
of coffee, sweetened, with milk.

Out the window,
snow-spruces step from their cobwebs.
Flurry of chickadees, feeding then gone.
A single cardinal stipples an empty branch –
one maple leaf lifted back.

I turn my blessings like photographs into the light;
over my shoulder the god of Not-Yet looks on:

Not-yet-dead, not-yet-lost, not-yet-taken.
Not-yet-shattered, not-yet-sectioned,
not-yet-strewn.

Ample litany, sparing nothing I hate or love,
not-yet-silenced, not-yet-fractured, not-yet- .

Not-yet-not.

I move my ear a little closer to that humming figure,
I ask him only to stay.

The Gift

When I offer the pear
and he takes it
with first whiskered lips
and then teeth
and soon it is no longer
fruit but goes into
betweenness and vanishment,
turning to pastern
and tail and good wall of the hoof
and small tithing of gold
for the pasture or fire roads –
for always where
there is offering, there is return;
when this happens
and he is careful even in greed,
even in the undignity
of his foolish – no, it must be
named true – his entirely goofy adoration
and long-tongued worship of pears;
when he knows what is pear,
what is hand, when he looks
in my face as he chews and the crush
slobbers out and foams bright as spent happiness
onto my foot, onto my sleeve,
as I bend then to lift him a wedge he has dropped;
when the heron holds steady in
contemplation not a few feet away,
its eyes once again closed like two stones
that have rested an hour in the sun
and gone back into leaning and dimness,
a little heat kept in them still;
when the late cars sweep by without pause,
without seeing, yet store in the
blue-shadowed beakers their own mild exchanges
of hidden, unwordable sweetness –

then the world is that actress from a Sanskrit poem,
whose greatness was showing two feelings at once:
The mercies are boundless. Every country is death's.

Three Foxes by the Edge of the Field at Twilight

One ran,
her nose to the ground,
a rusty shadow
neither hunting nor playing.

One stood; sat; lay down; stood again.

One never moved,
except to turn her head a little as we walked.

Finally we drew too close,
and they vanished.
The woods took them back as if they had never been.

I wish I had thought to put my face to the grass.

But we kept walking,
speaking as strangers do when becoming friends.

There is more and more I tell no one,
strangers nor loves.
This slips into the heart
without hurry, as if it had never been.

And yet, among the trees, something has changed.

Something looks back from the trees,
and knows me for who I am.

Leaf

Large as two hands together
still cupping rain,
yellow of amber stripped lightless,
scent of cold leather.
Nameless, one of ten thousand,
lifted without complaint or hope
to this painted table,
neither envelope nor letter.
Almost nothing. Yet before you,
words lie down in envy and silence,
switch their tails,
bury their damp, dark snouts between paws.

Studying *Wu Wei*, Muir Beach

There are days when you go
out into the bright spring fields
with the blue halter, the thick length
of rope with its sky-and-cloud braiding,
even the bucket of grain –
all corn-and-molasses sweetness,
the *maraca* sound of shaken seduction –
and the one you have gone for simply will not be caught.
It could be that the grass that day is too ripe.
It could be the mare who comes over, jutting her body
between his and yours. It could be
the wild-anise breeze that wanders in and out of his mane.
He might nip at the smallest mouthful,
but your hands' slightest rising – no matter how slow,
how cautious – breaks him away.
He doesn't have to run, though he knows he could.
Knows he is faster, stronger, less tied.
He knows he can take you or leave you in the dust.
But set aside purpose, leave the buckles and clasps
of intention draped over the fence, come forward
with both hands fully exposed, and he greedily eats.
Allows you to fondle his ears, scratch his neck, pull out
the broken half-carrot his soft-folded lips accept
tenderly from your palm. The mare edges close, and he
lays back one ear; the other stays pricked toward you,
in utmost attention. Whatever you came for,
this is what you will get: at best, a tempered affection
while red-tails circle and lupine shifts in the wind.
It is hard not to want to coerce a world that
takes what it pleases and walks away, but *Do not-doing*,
proposed Lao-tsu – and this horse. Today the world is tired.
It wants to lie down in green grass and stain its grey shoulders.
It wants to be left to study the non-human field,
to hold its own hungers, not yours, between its teeth.
Not words, but the sweetness of fennel. Not thought,
but the placid rituals of horse-dung and flies.

Nuzzling the festive altars from plantain to mustard,
from budded thistle to bent-stemmed rye. Feasting and flowering
and sleeping in every muscle, every muzzle, every bone it has.

Hope and Love

All winter
the blue heron
slept among the horses.
I do not know
the custom of herons,
do not know
if the solitary habit
is their way,
or if he listened for
some missing one –
not knowing even
that was what he did –
in the blowing
sounds in the dark.
I know that
hope is the hardest
love we carry.
He slept
with his long neck
folded, like a letter
put away.

Painting

There is a painting of it: an eighteenth-century miniature from the Kangra School of India, of the lovers, Krishna and Radha. In other paintings, they have sheltered together, stood under a canopy of invisibility among cows and the village girls who tend them. His hand has covered her breast. In other paintings, we have watched her prepare for him, behind the screen of a bedcloth held up by her friends. She is putting red dye on her nipples and the bottoms of her feet, while he looks down from an upstairs window, smiling. His body is blue, his flute's notes possess a god's effortless irresistibility. But here it is different. Though her eyes and mouth turn toward him with undeniable longing, she stops him with one raised hand. Inscribed on the page are his words, 'Hear me, hear what I ask,' and hers – they are simple, immediate – 'I hear, my Lord.' But still she is leaving, walking away. Though her torso turns back, her feet are already rising a little out of her slippers – the god, though not the viewer, can see the red dye as she goes. Under the silk of a sari so fine it could pass through the hoop of her earring, her nipples are standing.

The Fire

Again open
the book
of reds and golds.
Study the faces
of poppy and lion,
the bright-carpet
tapetum lucidum
of your own life.
What looks back
and seems to be burning,
is burning;
though not all the same:
in the moment
of turning away
from rain,
the day gives off –
red & gold –
the slightest scent
of peaches.
This too
so you might know things
as they are.
So you, who are
already walking within,
will come in.
Why else take up
the body's single candle,
if not to see
how everything is consumed?

Manners/Rwanda

They took the woman
and tied to one arm a child
to the other arm a child
to one leg a child
to the other leg a child –
you also read this in the paper –
and threw them all in.
No marks of damage, not one
on the five bodies,
which means of course
that they drowned,
which means of course
that she knew.
The river made its way
from higher ground toward lower
and carried them with decorum,
the way a river does,
it carries what it is given,
and because in the night
a border was crossed,
what was given then was
taken out with a pole.
It may have been untied
before being added
to the tally sheet with others
and given next
to the quicklime and earth,
but probably not.
There it will likely stay,
where it was carried,
the last contact
with anything living
a hand's continuing rising,
almost a waving,
almost a plea,
letting go after rolling it in.

The two beats of the fall
almost gentle,
a door being carefully opened,
quietly closed.
And though you too
are sickened, as even the river
is sickened, undrinkable now
with the human heart,
you also carry
what you were given with decorum.
Perhaps reminded later
by something mentioned
only in passing –
a large family,
a cat's toy of string –
you stop smiling a moment soon.
Across the table
someone notices,
but does not speak.
You watch his question rise
and seem to waver like a hand
about to act,
a hand about to change its mind,
then drop politely away.

Late Prayer

Tenderness does not choose its own uses.
It goes out to everything equally,
circling rabbit and hawk.
Look: in the iron bucket,
a single nail, a single ruby –
all the heavens and hells.
They rattle in the heart and make one sound.

Calmness

A woman tells of watching a hyena
eating her body.
Part of an arm first, then part of a leg.

It looked back at her
in a steadiness without malice or affection.

Though for months she had fed it,
watered it,
it swallowed looking.

And I think of those three sisters,
the Fates,
sharing their single eye.
Each spared seeing the whole.

How that tearless, almost-human blinking allowed them.

Respite

Day after quiet day passes.
I speak to no one besides the dog.
To her,
I murmur much I would not otherwise say.

We make plans,
then break them on a moment's whim.
She agrees;
though sometimes bringing
to my attention a small blue ball.

Passing the fig tree
I see it is
suddenly huge with green fruit,
which may ripen or not.

Near the gate,
I stop to watch
the sugar ants climb the top bar
and cross at the latch,
as they have now in summer for years.

In this way I study my life.
It is,
I think today,
like a dusty glass vase.

A little water,
a few flowers would be good,
I think;
but do nothing. Love is far away.
Incomprehensible sunlight falls on my hand.

Orange Oil in Darkness

The useful part
of things is elegance –
in mathematics, bridges.

Even in hedges
of ripe persimmons
or mandarin oranges,

elegance solves
for the minimum possible,
then dissolves.

The art is what is extra:
a fragrance pencilled in,
or long division's inescapable remainder.

Not quite unplanned for,
more the unexpected, impractical gift.
Not the figures traced

in the bridge's stanchions,
but the small
and lovely sounds they make in the wind.

Who drew that in?
Who could have?
For years now I've mistaken

art for beauty,
but it is not beauty.
Art lives in a plenitude more iron,

more empty, less demanding.
Art doesn't care,
except in moments of despair.

Those it lets pass, recognising weakness.

The Four-postered Beds of Mycenae

We were talking about inventions,
many of which were lying all around us.
Someone, for instance, had once invented
the table, perhaps trying three legs first,

and each of us wore on our feet
two invented socks, two shoes with their
laces usefully end-crimped in plastic,
their metal heel-taps and grommets.

It used to be said that the twelfth century
invented romantic love, but I have
always thought it unlikely, perhaps never
understanding what was meant by 'romantic'.

Paper was invented in many places,
using the skin of animals, ricestraw, clay,
tree bark, sand, ox-shoulder, and stone.
For the keepers of certain secrets,

the inside of a whole coconut is paper.
One man spoke of the numerous uses of copra,
and of lying many nights on the decks
of boats on which it was carried, overwhelmed

by its sweetness as by an idea
that cannot be escaped until invented.
Upstairs, in a corner, an invented walking cane
leaned quietly against an invented wall.

The difficult stairs, too, must have been
invented, someone deciding, before any code,
the exact parameters best suiting
the average foot, the usual leg, and a youthful

sense of vertiginous balance. Invention
is the opposite of balance: something leans
forward and falls into where there is nothing,
until a hammock appears, a string bag for groceries.

These catch the leaning mind, which straightens,
then begins, like a tree under ice,
to lean again. Some topple all the way over,
passing the work to others, who may use

the fallen lumber for an early model,
knocked together fast, with the fewest possible nails.
That way it may be disassembled and tried again.
Mostly the invented is disassembled, the shoes

uncobbled, the nails thrown back in an iron tub,
which is disassembled whole, into a horse trough,
and put out where the rain may disassemble it more.
An immaterial invention can be neither

knocked together nor disassembled,
yet some last as long as a Mycenaean palace –
certain rhythms, stories, or ways of knowing.
These inventions we ascribe to the blind,

as if only Homer unseeing could see so much,
and the sighted ones copy them hard, as I have here,
till their own vision starts to blur,
through wear or tears, into something invented.

Every family has its inventor, almost always
without patent; one's father invented recessed lights,
another's great uncle a kind of screw...
Pondering the immense fortunes we are not heir to,

we turn off the lamps in the room by pull-chain,
by turn-knob, by wall-switch (in this case two buttons,
one of which pops out when the other is pressed),
and by a small pole pushed through a lightbulb's base.

Genius, perhaps, is making anything
worth the world's stealing. Remembering Spender's
'I think continually of those who were truly great,'
I soap my face, brush teeth, lay head

on down-filled pillow wrapped in white cotton,
and lie in a bed with four posters –
not three, not five,
as the quatrain here is an unimprovable discovery.

Raised by that drowsy warmth above the cold floor,
above the cold, deep ground of the uninvented,
Spender's rhythms come strong in my ear,
and then the rhythms of others, as if nearby

some great ocean rushed the earth, retreated,
and rushed again, with a heavy, continual breaking
of all the words once hammered to full invention,
into a fully undisassemblable perfection.

Jasmine

'Almost the twenty-first century' –
how quickly the thought will grow dated,
even quaint.

Our hopes, our future,
will pass like the hopes and futures of others.

And all our anxieties and terrors,
nights of sleeplessness,
griefs,
will appear then as they truly are –

Stumbling, delirious bees in the tea scent of jasmine.

III.

THE SWEETNESS OF APPLES, OF FIGS

The Sweetness of Apples, of Figs

In Bellini's painting,
the usual angel
is not present,
only a man
opening his chest
to the world
of simple sheep
and goose and hare
in the strange light.
Book and skull,
the two wooden sandals,
lie forgotten
behind the open-lattice door.
Even his pin-pricked
hands, it seems, forgotten.
Again the holy striving
has given way
to ordinary joy.
It is mostly blues,
a little reddish-brown,
some green.

Noon Bells, Lake Como

Minutes apart,
from every side of the lake
they name the hour,
as if time
here were many, not one –

A story told this way
in Menaggio, but in Cadenabbia,
different –
'A cow? It was a goat,
with my own eyes I saw it!'

Changing Everything

I was walking again
in the woods,
a yellow light
was sifting all I saw.

Willfully,
with a cold heart,
I took a stick,
lifted it to the opposite side
of the path.

There, I said to myself,
that's done now.
Brushing one hand against the other,
to clean them
of the tiny fragments of bark.

Bees

In every instant, two gates.
One opens to fragrant paradise, one to hell.
Mostly we go through neither.

Mostly we nod to our neighbor,
lean down to pick up the paper,
go back into the house.

But the faint cries – ecstasy, horror?
Or did you think it the sound
of distant bees,
making only the thick honey of this good life?

Mulberries

By the time
the low branches
ripen the pigeons are fat,
and can be generous.
Just so, let
the gods take what they want
of this world and its high nectars –
Know they will leave
the stews and the nipple's erectness,
the unguarded, late-sweetening
pleasures.

Mele in Gabbia

The pastry
is dusted with sugar.
The slices of apple inside,
just sour enough.

The name,
'apples in a cage'.

I eat them
in this good place –
the pastry warm,
a little bit chewy,
the linen
impeccably white –
and consider.

Wine Grapes for Breakfast

Sweet
at first
on the tongue,
hours later
the red grapes
still sting,
as if trying
to tell me something –
what the hook
tells the fish
perhaps,
or the wand
or stick hears
before conductor
or mule driver
brings it down.

The Bearded Woman

Each time she noticed,
she had meant
to pluck the three black hairs,
but the days were short;
her fingers touched her chin
then forgot.
Thus fatigue grew curling into wisdom.

Lying

He puts his brush to the canvas,
with one quick stroke
unfolds a bird from the sky.
Steps back, considers.
Takes pity.
Unfolds another.

A Month of Days and Nights

Days that could have
been anything,
nights that could have been anything,
turned with the leaves.

Then, someone played
the piano –
halting,
unpractised, and perfect.

I listened to pity
and lowered my head in shame.
Ashamed not at my tears,
or even at what had been wasted,
but to have been dry-eyed so long.

Love amid Owl Cries

It is not
the altar that matters,
not that,
nor the shape
that is found there.
The ghostly ideas
come and go, one after another.
But the place endures.
The fact that there is a door.

The Clock

Night pond,
its few leaves
floating:
absence-of-stars,
drifting over the surface.

But even
fallen things
disrupt each other.
Beauty, griefs turn over.
The leaves move
all night, slowly,
until they again are red.

Each Moment a White Bull Steps Shining into the World

If the gods bring to you
a strange and frightening creature,
accept the gift
as if it were one you had chosen.

Say the accustomed prayers,
oil the hooves well,
caress the small ears with praise.

Have the new halter of woven silver
embedded with jewels.
Spare no expense, pay what is asked,
when a gift arrives from the sea.

Treat it as you yourself
would be treated,
brought speechless and naked
into the court of a king.

And when the request finally comes,
do not hesitate even an instant –

Stroke the white throat,
the heavy, trembling dewlaps
you've come to believe were yours,
and plunge in the knife.

Not once
did you enter the pasture
without pause,
without yourself trembling.
That you came to love it, that was the gift.

Let the envious gods take back what they can.

Letting What Enters Enter

Even in January rains
the blossoms open –
absence and longing
are also the plum-fragrant spring.
As the woman with her
sign and cart of rags is spring,
beside the highway, stepping slowly
through the undimmed flower of her life.
'What I now most want to happen
in my raving heart, make it happen' –
Sappho's cry to the goddess.
Who knows if that prayer was answered?
Each part holds the rest in the chill
spring rain and the silence; let one animal
eat from your hand and the whole herd comes.
But the woman was not beautiful
or whole in her own heart's raving,
and she forgave me nothing that I love.

Lake and Maple

I want to give myself
utterly
as this maple
that burned and burned
for three days without stinting
and then in two more
dropped off every leaf;
as this lake that,
no matter what comes
to its green-blue depths,
both takes and returns it.
In the still heart,
that refuses nothing,
the world is twice-born –
two earths wheeling,
two heavens,
two egret reaching
down into subtraction;
even the fish
for an instant doubled,
before it is gone.
I want the fish.
I want the losing it all
when it rains and I want
the returning transparence.
I want the place
by the edge-flowers where
the shallow sand is deceptive,
where whatever
steps in must plunge,
and I want that plunging.
I want the ones
who come in secret to drink
only in early darkness,
and I want the ones
who are swallowed.

I want the way
this water sees without eyes,
hears without ears,
shivers without will or fear
at the gentlest touch.
I want the way it
accepts the cold moonlight
and lets it pass,
the way it lets
all of it pass
without judgment or comment.
There is a lake,
Lalla Ded sang, no larger
than one seed of mustard,
that all things return to.
O heart, if you
will not, cannot, give me the lake,
then give me the song.

Knowing Nothing

Love is not the reason.
Love is the lure,
the thin goat staked out in the clearing.

The lion has stalked
the village for a long time.
It does not want the goat,
who stands thin and bleating,
tied to its bit of wood.

The goat is not the reason.
The reason is the lion,
whose one desire is to enter –
Not the goat, which is
only the lure, only excuse,
but the one burning life
it has hunted for a long time
disguised as hunger. Disguised as love.
Which is not the reason.

Or would you think
that the bones of a lion reason?
Would you think that the tongue?
The lion does not want the goat,
it wants only to live. Alone if it must.
In pain if it must. Knowing nothing.
Like the goat, it wants only to live.
Like love. Or would you think that the heart?

If the Rise of the Fish

If for a moment
the leaves fell upward,
if it seemed a small flock
of brown-orange birds
circled over the trees,
if they circled then scattered each in
its own direction for the lost seed
they had spotted in tall, gold-chequered grass.
If the bloom of flies on the window
in morning sun, if their singing insistence
on grief and desire. If the fish.
If the rise of the fish.
If the blue morning held in the glass of the window,
if my fingers, my palms. If my thighs.
If your hands, if my thighs.
If the seeds, among all the lost gold of the grass.
If your hands on my thighs, if your tongue.
If the leaves. If the singing fell upward. If grief.
For a moment if singing and grief.
If the blue of the body fell upward, out of our hands.
If the morning held it like leaves.

Reading Chinese Poetry Before Dawn

Sleepless again,
I get up.
A cold rain
beats at the windows.
Holding my coffee,
I ponder Tu Fu's
overturned wine glass.
At his window, snow,
twelve hundred years fallen;
under his hand,
black ink not yet dry.
'Letters are useless,' it reads.
The poet is old, alone,
his woodstove is empty.
The fame of centuries
casts off no heat.
In his verse, I know,
is a discipline
lost to translation;
here, only the blizzard remains.

The Poet

She is working now, in a room
not unlike this one,
the one where I write, or you read.
Her table is covered with paper.
The light of the lamp would be
tempered by a shade, where the bulb's
single harshness might dissolve,
but it is not, she has taken it off.
Her poems? I will never know them,
though they are the ones I most need.
Even the alphabet she writes in
I cannot decipher. Her chair –
Let us imagine whether it is leather
or canvas, vinyl or wicker. Let her
have a chair, her shadeless lamp,
the table. Let one or two she loves
be in the next room. Let the door
be closed, the sleeping ones healthy.
Let her have time, and silence,
enough paper to make mistakes and go on.

White Curtain in Sunlight and Wind

More and more
wanting to learn
how to leave things be.
To live as the old Dutch painters
looked at a fish:
all of it eaten but leaving no sign.
Or if so much cannot be given,
then to enter as Chuang-tzu's butcher
entered an ox – slipping completely through;
each cut, sinew and fat, sharpening
the knife. Nothing taken, or left behind.
Heart returned to the granite mountains of its home.
After, it could almost walk away.

A Room

A room does not turn its back on grief.
Anger does not excite it.
Before desire, it neither responds
nor draws back in fear.

Without changing expression,
it takes
and gives back;
not a tuft in the mattress alters.

Windowsills evenly welcome
both heat and cold.
Radiators speak or fall silent as they must.

Doors are not equivocal,
floorboards do not hesitate or startle.
Impatience does not stir the curtains,
a bed is neither irritable nor rapacious.

Whatever disquiet we sense in a room
we have brought there.

And so I instruct my ribs each morning,
pointing to hinge and plaster and wood –

 You are matter, as they are.
 See how perfectly it can be done.
 Hold, one day more, what is asked.

One Penny

Everything draws back,
not so much a season
as a lack.

The maple sap burns low,
unfanned. Pondwater,
ice-blown, retreats to a corner.

The plowed drive's shoe-string
drops on a half-sketched map,
dirty, untied.

A rabbit-crossing
hops to the other side –
soft fold in the paper, blurring.

Movement I can't quite catch:
the fourth deer
of the afternoon, bounding away.

Where does she bed? There is
no shelter, only trunks too thin
themselves to stop a wind,

their colored leaves
long swept off, or scrubbed,
or whittled.

One faded splinter
rattles from a twig like a cough.
Even winter's used up –

no bright fierceness, no falling snow.
An icicle drips
in watered-whiskey sunlight,

the heart tips south like a tin cup.

Cabin

A frozen wasps' nest
stalls
beneath the place
the roof wears out
over a wall.

The window casements
crack,
too empty even to
be lonely.

A small grief
really,
only big enough for one.

Now it stands
like the actor in Noh Zeami wrote of –

His secret is having
something he knows but does not say.

He is old,
he has almost forgotten
what has been broken.
It will not be kissed away.

The Illuminist

Even in his glass cabin you can see
the man driving the snowplow
is whistling, happy. He races
one road, then the next, moving new snow.

A monk patiently hammering gold-leaf,
before him the world grows pliably, steadily brighter.

And if more will fall again tonight,
no matter.
He will put on his hat, his gloves,
and make again order.

All day the plow's sound rises,
a pre-Gregorian chanting singing its singer.
Gold of winter sun grows thinner and thinner.

Now
he can lay it right in with the little plow.

The scriptorium darkens over white vellum.
His puttering ink-stroke, lengthening,
glows.

Broken-off Twig Budding Out in the Path

Only the slightest thaw,
and something plops
in the water that clears.

It may be nothing
that swims,
nothing that hops, or hopes.

Edge-ice falling in.
Something that happens
and simply stops.

Or it may be a thing
like this stick –
its red buds swelling out

in spite of what it
ought to know,
in spite of where it ought to be.

Some quickened water sprout,
separate
beyond naming in its early spring.

Blind Fate Walking on Ice in the Woods

The mildest slope of her guide dog's
shoulders
makes a difference. The yaw

of the wind in the harness
makes a difference.
Everything here is ice-clear,
even to her.

I balance on my eyes. The rest of us do –
vision's two canes
like a walker set down before us.

Now she is passing
close enough almost to kiss.

Cold scent of wool, of soup.

Her life.

If you looked into her face,
you would fall in an instant.

Matter and Spirit

A shadow empties itself into a river.
No one sees.
But the cloth for washing the bodies of the dead
softens, gentles a little.
Neither the cloth nor the body feels this,
yet it matters. Someone else, you see, is there,
in the blunt and the blind of grace –
Someone stands silent,
listening, the looped cotton held in her hand.

Spell To Be Said Upon Waking

Trout's maculate body,
delible house of the wasps' nests,
white face of the horse –

Draw close.
A shadow closes your foxgrass,
lichens your boulders.

Cloudy the vow of the leaf in the water.

Lion, where is your hunger?
Come tortoise, come river, eat.

Desire, walk easily now through the wild net
of birchwood in rain,
on mountain-back carry the brindled immeasurable day.

Spell To Be Said Before Sleep

Each pot now hang bright
on the black peg;
grief, mend the owl's wing further.

Who will follow her singing
into the river, into the mountain?
Now it is one note, now two,
the moon hurried into the snow.

Shines back the breath of the mare.
Lucent,
dreaming the mountain of moment and moment,
black tail bless the dark.

Slender the bones
of the forelegs all night keeping watch,
stand over the one who is sleeping.
Stand over the owl.
Three times brush the tail of the darkness.

One stone in the bed of the River of Heaven
is the mare.
One is the owl. One is the singing.

Guard them, o earth, in your travels.

Spell To Be Said After Illness

Crabapple holding in arms
what almost has
vanished,
selvage and leaf-lavish open.

Pumpkin seed in the hand,
lick the salt after.
What remains, after.
Bowl fill with woodpecker's shavings of cedar.

Door of the beak, release attic.
Voice remain fragrant.
Love hold the lungs again open.

By the bed, here.
By silence and whiteness,
by staying.
Carved scent of orange-oil, open.

By rise of the woodpecker's question,
of crabapple fruiting,
clasp now this room that is given.

Open with flood what is given,
once again fragrant and here.

Spell for Inviting-in the New Soul

Shy one,
small donkey, come forward.
Let world be cradle.

Fish drifting, enter weight gladly.
Trust passage.

If suffering will chant you,
if terror,
in pine dark, deer breathing.
In sea-bench's sorrow gills salt-light.

Know owl-cries your forelock.

Know leaf-scent, know cities, know rivers,
doorways stand open.
In ice-grip, know muskrat's strong swimming.
Let asking.

Let losing and breaking, let weather.
Let entrance entirely.
Desires bray sweet in the ladders of loudness.

Shy one, small donkey, trust hoof-fall.
Seeds wait to ride on your ankles,
five baskets
of apple sleep guardian.

The bridle placed heavy wears bell-sounds.
Agreeing come forward.

Spell To Be Said Upon Departure

What was come here to do
having finished,
shelves of the water lie flat.

Copper the leaves of the doorsill,
yellow and falling.
Scarlet the bird that is singing.

Vanished the labor, here walls are.
Completed the asking.
Loosing the birds there is water.

Having eaten the pears.
Having eaten
the black figs, the white figs. Eaten the apples.

Table be strewn.
Table be strewn with stems,
table with peelings of grapefruit and pleasure.

Table be strewn with pleasure,
what was here to be done having finished.

Lion and Angel Dividing the Maple Between Them

Easy to see
that the lion and angel
are one visitation,
but how do you come
to offer your throat to either?
In autumn, the trees
learn to drop off
both their disguises,
what finally fills them is simple.
The heart's deepest
affections will equally be devoured.
And still we go ankle deep
into that carnage, lifting first one,
then another part up to the light.
As if we were looking for something simple.
As if what we wanted
were not the thing that falls.

Milk

From time to time the placid
shrugs its shoulders –
earthquakes, for instance –

but still the world
depends
on placid things' resistance.

The fire requires
its trees,
the sea its hem of boulders,

the wind
without its halls
would howl in silence;

for everything that
flares up, something lowers
itself, digs in

for an existence
in the long haul, slows.
It may well be the placid knows

its worth. The cow whose
calf was taken
eats again – but do not guess

too quickly at the meaning
in the red hips' unbent squareness,
the large-jawed head

half-buried in the grass:
with each fly's weightless
bite, the thick skin shivers.

The placid, unlike us,
lives in the moment.
Something must;

like chairs,
or painted dressers,
on an earth where loss

is so all present
that we drink it without thinking,
blue-white in its early morning glass.

Talc

When you phoned I was far, and sleeping,
but they brought me the message and I ran,
I ran to the phone where you were,
you were speaking, we two were speaking,
when I ran back to the room I no longer
knew we would speak again. Twenty minutes
and I was gone, there was a plane,
and another, there was a friend who took
me to you, you were asleep. I didn't know
there was still any question, I only learned
later, everything later, weeks later I was
still frightened of all that I learned.
I swear though I knew it was there I scarcely
saw the hose taped to your mouth, its ridges
that breathed in case you did not; scarcely saw
the twin tubes coming out of your chest or
the blood running through them and into the pump
that returned to your wrist, quietly, steadily,
what belonged there. The slenderer tubes
that entered the side of your neck I scarcely
noticed; not the empty ones waiting for something
not needed, not the ones drawing fluids
from three labelled bags. They had washed you,
I barely noticed the yellow stains and the blood
that remained on your skin. They had cut you,
I did not see the bandages holding the length
of the chest, they lay where I should have been
lying, I did not understand. I did not see
the wounds on your side where some scalpel or saw
had been dropped or some heated or iced tool
had burned. The monitor's chiming was nothing,
someone would come, they would turn it off.
The slash stapling the crease of your thigh was
nothing. When the nurse turned the white valve
near the collarbones' nest before opening one
on the wrist, there was not one cell of my body

that needed to understand. I barely felt the bars
where my hand fitted into your hand, the rail
that days afterward still tracked my cheek.
The urine that drained to the sack below us must
have been warm, I must have touched it, I should
have known it was warm with your warmth but I did not.
I waited. I knew that the sweetness I smelled
on your body was powder, was baby powder, I did
not understand, but I knew they had given you back
to this world for a second time and I waited
for you to agree. I waited for you to open your eyes,
a first time, another, another. I waited until
you were sure, until every part of you stayed.

Each Happiness Ringed by Lions

Sometimes when
I take you into my body
I can almost see them – patient, circling.
Almost glimpse the moving shadow of the tail,
almost hear the hushed pad of retracted claws.
It is the moment – of this I am certain –
when they themselves are least sure.
It is the moment they could almost let us go free.

Three Times My Life Has Opened

Three times my life has opened.
Once, into darkness and rain.
Once, into what the body carries at all times within it and starts
 to remember each time it enters the act of love.
Once, to the fire that holds all.
These three were not different.
You will recognise what I am saying or you will not.
But outside my window all day a maple has stepped from her leaves
 like a woman in love with winter, dropping the colored silks.
Neither are we different in what we know.
There is a door. It opens. Then it is closed. But a slip of light
 stays, like a scrap of unreadable paper left on the floor,
 or the one red leaf the snow releases in March.

from

THE OCTOBER PALACE

(1988–1994)

The Kingdom

At times
the heart
stands back
and looks at the body,
looks at the mind,
as a lion
quietly looks
at the not-quite-itself,
not-quite-another,
moving of shadows and grass.

Wary, but with interest,
considers its kingdom.

Then seeing
all that will be,
heart once again enters –
enters hunger, enters sorrow,
enters finally losing it all.
To know, if nothing else,
what it once owned.

I.

WHAT THE HEART WANTS

What the Heart Wants

See then
what the heart wants,
that pliable iron
sprung to the poppy's redness,
the honey's gold, winged
as the heron-lit water is:
by reflecting.
As an aged elephant answers
the slightest, first gesture of hand,
it puts itself at the mercy –
utterly docile, the forces
that brought it there vanished,
fold into fold.
And the old-ice ivory, the unstartlable
black of the eye that has travelled so far
with the fringed, peripheral howdah
swaying behind, look mildly back
as it swings the whole bulk of the body
close to the ground. Over and over
it does this, bends to what asks.
Whatever asks, heart kneels and offers to bear.

Each Step

Nowhere on this earth
is it not a place where the lovers
turn lightly in sleep in each other's arms,
the blue pastures of dusk flowing gladly
into the dawn.

Nowhere that is not reached by the scent
of good bread
through an open window,
by the flash of fish in the flashing of summer streams,
or the trees unfolding their praises –
apricots, pears – of the winter-chill nights.

Briefly, briefly, we see it, and forget.
As if the spell were too powerful to hold on the tongue,
as if we preferred the weight to the prize –

Like a horse
that carries on his own back
the sacks of oats he will need, unsuspecting,
looking always ahead,
over the mountains, to where sweet springs lie.

He remembers this much from his youth,
the taste of things, cold and pure –
while the water-sound sings on and on, unlistened to,
in his ears;
while each step is nothing less than the glistening
river-body reentering home.

The Shadow

That morning, sitting quietly,
I knew for a moment
the unlocked transom of the body:
how the rib-staves bridge a sheer lake
the same within them as without;
how the wrist bones spill the sky's austere
unwaking when the crickets have been still
for hours and the wrens' low whistles
and rasp-tongued bluejays have not yet begun.
Across the continent it was full light,
and a man I loved was tending the body of his mother.
Not the one already ash, but the one of paper,
slipped into drawers, packed into trunks, left behind.
His fingers were turning the smoothed-flat pages,
the middles' ink-dark thicket to be passed through
as the black scribblings of birth-ink and death-ink
must be passed through, and the edges white because the body
has its limits, there are things unspoken between mothers
and sons, and when he tried to tell me,
later, what it was like, there were silences too,
between us and within us. Listen, he said then,
and I did, while he held the receiver's open mouthpiece
toward the east. In each of our bodies, the sea
swung close, then farther off, on its watery stem.
By then, it was night again for us both, another day paid out
in bolted cloth. 'Memory,' she'd once written, 'is like the shadow
of a building, longest just when it turns to disappear....'
Still we stayed on the open phone line hearing
the beating, breaking, scoured-out chimes of wave-scrub –
diamond and black the space between them, empty, vast,
I almost could see it – for a long, silent time, remembering her.

Cycladic Figure:
The Harp Player (*ca.* 3000 B.C.E.)

Body out of whose being
Orpheus stepped,
already you
were a whole, already
you had become perfection.
Your face is tipped
upward in simple, oval listening,
as all of your kind's
were tipped upward –
like a blind cup to the blind sun,
yet something
passing between them.
Your hands are unmoving,
the harp's white triangle
balances empty above your thighs,
it is the same
substance as the thighs,
it is the thighs' singing, shown.
We have grown more modest:
singing comes now through the ears,
the head bends downward
in concentration,
like pendulous flowers' heads
from long standing in rain,
or perhaps from the weight
of too much seeing, too much seen.
Your marble is
flawless, continuous, seamless.
When I look at you
you do not look back,
your only direction is inner,
everything enters.
And so the Other
had to step out of you,
into desire,
into Orpheus and incompletion.

The earth –
how could you know this,
who had no ears, who had no eyes? –
wanting so much to be heard,
even the broken-tongued grieving,
that instant clamor,
seemed to it plausible, lovely.

History as the Painter Bonnard

Because nothing is ever finished
the painter would shuffle, *bonnarding*,
into galleries, museums, even the homes of his patrons,
with hidden palette and brush:
overscribble drapery and table with milk jug or fattened pear,
the clabbered, ripening colors of second sight.

Though he knew with time the pentimenti rise –
half-visible, half brine-swept fish, their plunged shapes
pocking the mind – toward the end, only revision mattered:
to look again, more deeply, harder, clearer,
the one redemption granted us to ask.

This, we say, is what we meant to say. This. This.
– as the kiss, the sorrowful murmur,
may cover a child's bruises, if not retract the blow.
While a woman in Prague asks softly, in good English
for the camera, 'But who will give us back these twenty years?'

Ah love, o history, forgive
the squandered light and flung-down rags of chances,
old choices drifted terribly awry.
And world, self-portrait never right, receive this gift –
shuffling, spattered, stubborn,
something nameless opens in the heart: to touch
with soft-bent sable, ground-earth pigment, seed-clear oil,
the rounding, bright-fleshed present, if not the past.

The kissed child puts his hand at last back into his mother's,
though it is not the same;
her fine face neither right nor wrong, only thoroughly his.

(November–December, 1989)

167

The Wedding

Nothing is lost, nothing created: everything is transformed.

ANTOINE LAURENT LAVOISIER,
Elements of Chemistry (1789)

The high windows stream with fish,
the gold luck of carp,
the tiny silver luck of minnows,
while the earth gives back her buried wealth
of skunks and star-crossed badgers:
pure stripes of seeing unfurl themselves
out of moonlight, and the dark bodies
follow as closely as boat follows sail
and know no harm will come to them in their wholeness.
All beings rise, uncaught, for this beginning.
Cousin Death joins a table at the wedding,
the white cloth gleams, the waiting plates,
all are made welcome.
Mother War smooths the silk of her dress,
she feels young and will dance again, after years,
with her husband, Pity.
Still the guests are arriving, carrying gifts:
small appliances, vases, a thick set of towels,
lamps of heaviest brass.
They say each other's names, Charity, Hope, and ask
of nieces and nephews off to school.
A rabbit edges near, outside the glass.
On the river a barge floats softly, its tugs at slack;
night herons and pelicans preen, an iron bell warms
with the slow ringing fire of rust and the barge imperceptibly
lowers. Imagine nothing created, what it might look like,
try to envision such peace.
Now see the dark-shelled flowers of thought unmade,
the petals of Little Boy unassembled,
the plague-poxed donkeys unflung over city walls, the dead
undead, the survivors unlonely. Or think of a world
in which nothing is lost, its heaped paintings,
the studded statues keeping their jewels.

Now see this very world, where all is transformed,
quick as a child who cries and then laughs in her crying –
now ingot, now blossoming ash,
now table, now suckling lamb on that table.
How each thing meets the other as itself, the luminous, changing
mirror of itself – mercuric oxide tipped from flask to flask,
first two, then one, wedded for life in that vow.

A Plenitude

Even from a book of aging plates
these frescoes' intricate traceries
dazzle the eye
with their crazed-china, fourteenth-century glaze:
in gold walls, gold vines
flicker and rise in intertwining diamonds,
in red bedding, damask blooms –
Each swath of floor or cloth
a plenitude that binds,
each peak-roofed canopy
a worked geometry of laddered tiles
or stones whose almost-symmetry is repetition
as in nature, invented always new.
For these storied rooms seem not so much
built up by plan as breathed,
until at times they seem to break
as if from sheer exuberance to dapplings
spilled out selfless as animal pelts
or roots whose autumn pattern nets a hill
against the rain's entreating beat to join in falling.
Other times, though,
they seem delicately revealed,
as if some smooth and outer rind had been peeled back
to show the web of sweet-celled seed on seed
that is the world.
But there is the story, too,
of a young painter meeting the envoy of a Pope.
Asked for a work by which his art
could be weighed against others', he dipped his stylus –
with great courtesy, according to Vasari –
in red ink, and drew a single, perfect O.
Shocked, the messenger asked, 'Will this be all?'
Young Giotto (whose deerfly his teacher had tried in vain
to brush from a painting) replied,
'It is enough and more.'

Narcissus: Tel Aviv, Baghdad, San Francisco;
February 1991

And then the precise
opening everywhere of the flowers,
which live after all in their own time.
It seemed they were oblivious but they were not,
they included it all, the nameless explosions
and the oil fires in every cell, the white petals
like mirrors opening in a slow-motion coming-apart
and the stems, the stems rising like green-flaring missiles,
like smoke, like the small sounds shaken
from those who were beaten – like dust from a carpet –
into the wind and the spring-scented rain.
They opened because it was time and they had no choice,
as the children were born in that time and that place
and became what they would without choice, or with only
a little choice, perhaps, for the lucky, the foolish or brave.
But precise and in fact wholly peaceful the flowers opened,
and precise and peaceful the earth: opened because it was asked.
Again and again it was asked and earth opened –
flowered and fell – because what was falling had asked
and could not be refused, as the seabirds that ask the green surface
to open are not refused but are instantly welcomed,
that they may enter and eat –
As soon refuse, battered and soaking, the dark mahogany rain.

'Perceptibility Is a Kind of Attentiveness'
– Novalis

It is not enough
to see only the beauty,
this light
that pools aluminum
in the winter branches of apple –
it is only a sign
of the tree looking out
from the tree,
of the light looking
back at the light,
the long-celled attention.
The leaves too,
and the fruit, distract
in their sweetness and rustling.
As snow distracts,
covering the tree's looking out
with its own,
and the fragrance of blossoms.
Only stripped
of its multiple selves,
its many fabrics of loveliness,
does the tree's eye
step into a form
we can see with our own,
the black roots twisting down
from the heart,
ours equally whorled,
equally silent,
a flood-swept corridor keeping
no vision but life's –
A mirror looks into a mirror,
colorless, plain,
what flows between them
passes like water through a net.
A dragon-palace, but what dragon?

Its flowing scales of emerald,
emerald water;
its roaring rush,
tide-rush of water;
the treasure – oh even the treasure –
treasure of water.

In the Year Eight Hundred

Because of bad weather,
fever,
an unusual number
of fires, the Crown Prince Sawara
was (in the year eight hundred,
and after great debate)
declared Emperor of Japan,
though murdered five years before.

It is said that his spirit
was much appeased
and thereafter the kingdom flourished:
even the silkworms' castings
grew whiter, more strong,
on the mulberry leaves of the new court.
Poems were written,
songs of rejoicing sung,
the proper ceremonies enacted in darkened rooms,

and later, his power secured,
the Great One retired;
in order, it was proclaimed,
to better contemplate the various fates of man.

A Recurring Possibility

Asked on the icy steps
what she concealed in her mantle,
Elizabeth of Hungary
felt compelled to show her husband
the eggs, bread, and meat.
Instead, white roses,
red – though it was mid-December –
spilled from the heavy cloth.
It is in this miracle she is most often painted.
After the Landgrave's death,
her confessor grew more and more strict.
Took from her her four children.
Took from her the happiness of good works.
When she died at twenty-four,
the poor had returned to their hunger,
her back was cobwebbed with scars,
her last word was *Silence*.
What would it be to live fully
in these our bodies? It is almost
eight centuries later, it is raining.
The ordinary roses, whose fragrance is earthly,
like her have nothing to say.

Floor

The nails, once inset, rise to the surface –
or, more truly perhaps, over years
the boards sink down to meet what holds them.
Worn, yes, but not worn through:
the visible work reveals itself in iron,
to be pounded down again, for what we've declared
the beautiful to be.

The Hawk Cry

I do not know
what brought it to the middle
of the room made warm by the fire
I had lit before breakfast.
The day before it had run, seeing me,
out of my sight, but now even the sharp
involuntary animal-warning I made, seeing it,
did not seem to reach it at all.
Perhaps it was sick, or starving,
trapped in this place for days with nothing to eat
but paper. Perhaps it was simply old.
It lay with its eyes pressed closed
and seemed to concentrate hard on whatever it was.
Not knowing what better to do, I nudged it
gently as I could onto the dustpan;
and once, twice, the eyes opened, then shut back down.
I just took it out, rolled that softly pondering
body into the grass.
A few minutes later watched it move off into the weeds.
All day the world went on about its business.
Squirrels carrying acorns, the two thin cats
at their accustomed hour crossing the wash of the sun.
I read and slept a little, drank more coffee.
Why would a dying mouse – whether it lived or died
it must have been dying, to act as it did –
come out that way into the open?
To borrow a few minutes' life from the woodstove's heat?
To better offer itself to the one it must have known
would take it quickly, surely, for its own purpose?
Or was it a simpler surrender even than that,
almost magnetic, to some incomprehensible trust?
It did not fight at all when I gave it
to the broom's yellow stiffness, or lend its assent.
It simply let what happened happen, and even
watched a little as it did.

Autumn

Again the wind
flakes gold-leaf from the trees
and the painting darkens –
as if a thousand penitents
kissed an icon
till it thinned
back to bare wood,
without diminishment.

What Falls

Today, what falls is wavering
from rain to snow to rain, shifting from sound
to silence and back through moments
when only the breath of invisible waters
beads on the windows and eaves and makes its way down.
It does not want to come into the audible music,
the palace where courtiers walk softly in slippers
across the tiled floors.
It wants us to come out, and can wait.
Old love falls in rope-strands of hair from a barber's apron,
quince blossoms fall while attempting to follow the rising new moon,
mutterings fall from our feet when we walk –
first in the pattered notes of the very young,
tuneless and mild,
later the shuffling speech of the very old:
both aimless and pure in their vision of nowhere to go,
a world which is all destination.
Only between do we walk with determined purpose,
pacing the mapped-out roads of our century's life
as we must, though we are wrong to, and even, sometimes,
know we are wrong: the map incorrect and cruelly drawn,
its colors ugly.... Now, as I listen,
the falling has changed from not quite the one,
not quite the other, to fully silent, and snow.
Thought that rises like roses out of the intricate carpets
will quiet like this, its reds and blues
muted to flesh-tones, its stylised thorns undone.
The kingdom will fall to a different ruler,
whose armies will go. The halls of the palace, mutable,
mute, will begin to surrender, wild apples will grow,
while somewhere, softly, plows start up their muzzled groan –
What falls is independent angels, flowers, stones, the fragile
lace of colored light through glass, the body's window.
What falls is also snow and only snow, a cold precipitate of
 watered air,
but crystalline and visible, as we are.

The Door

A note waterfalls steadily
through us,
just below hearing.

Or this early light
streaming through dusty glass:
what enters, enters like that,
unstoppable gift.

And yet there is also the other,
the breath-space held between any call
and its answer –

In the querying
first scuff of footstep,
the wood-owls' repeating,
the two-counting heart:

A little sabbath,
minnow whose brightness silvers past time.

The rest-note,
unwritten,
hinged between worlds,
that precedes change and allows it.

II.

THE ANSWERING YES

1973

That winter we took turns stepping into
the barely started mornings to turn ignitions
until they caught, complaining roughly
of the cold, then ran
back to finish our coffee, cereal, toast,
while, chokes pulled full out,
exhaust poured white across the glass
that kept us warm...
We'd named them: Big Mama Tomato, Snooze.
Each was our first, as we
were each other's first, in the farmhouse
for rent for the first time
in forty years surrounded by soybeans.
We'd whited-over the pink room the son
had painted when he returned crazed with Vietnam.
We'd made the man come back for the thin black lab
left chained in the yard.
The thirteen cats stayed, soon more, all wild.
Our own would come to the window by way of
a three-story oak and moss-shingled porch roof,
to mew us awake and them in every day:
Kesey & Mountain Girl, scrawling their signatures
snow-mornings on the quilt.
We nailed planks from the old barns onto the walls
by our bed, scraped a dozen layers of peeling paper
from the next room – the older they got,
the more lovely. That one we made cheerful yellow,
where I wrote the wildly sad poems of the very young.
When we got to the farm you took a tractor, I loaded
my van with sacks of produce & drove off.
Kip supervised us all: the Peace Corps vet, the kids

just out of school. Picking his peaches that summer
the best work I've done, the closest to Paradise
I've seen, ladder-propped in his trees.
All sold now, gone, his farm, the one we lived at,
the groundfall cider, the cars.
Us too, of course, long shaken free, though
I still cook bluefish the way you taught me, and carrots.
I thought I would love you forever – and, a little, I may,
in the way I still move toward a crate, knees bent,
or reach for a man: as one might stretch
for the three or four fruit that lie in the sun at the top
of the tree; too ripe for any moment but this,
they open their skin at first touch, yielding sweetness,
sweetness and heat, and in me, each time since,
the answering yes.

Happiness

I think it was from the animals
that St Francis learned
it is possible to cast yourself
on the earth's good mercy and live.
From the wolf who cast off
the deep fierceness of her first heart
and crept into the circle of sunlight
in full wariness and wolf-hunger,
and was fed, and lived; from the birds
who came fearless to him until he
had no choice but return that courage.
Even the least amoeba touched on all sides
by the opulent Other, even the baleened
plankton fully immersed in their fate –
for what else might happiness be
than to be porous, opened, rinsed through
by the beings and things?
Nor could he forget those other companions,
the shifting, ethereal, shapeless:
Hopelessness, Desperateness, Loneliness,
even the fire-tongued Anger –
for they too waited with the patient Lion,
the glossy Rooster, the drowsy Mule, to step
out of the trees' protection and come in.

This Love

Most lovely of the things I loved and lose: the sunlight;
next, bright stars, the moon,
ripe gourds, the fruit of apple trees, the pears.
PRAXILLA (*fl.* 440 B.C.E.)

A lucky woman,
Praxilla, to have tasted
the cucumber missed more severely than gold.
And lucky, whoever learns there is only one loss,
the bracelets glinting heavy and warm on the wrist,
fastened there for the first time
by a lover's hand,
and the lizard-cool fruit growing outside the door,
cobbled and rivered with all the green waters of earth.
Exiles, too, must know something
of how it will be, the ones who say not 'I miss Paris'
but 'Paris is missing me' –
For it is the other which stays, we who depart,
and any piece of it, even the smallest, would more than suffice.
As lifting a single silk thread, the whole cloth must come,
if the silk is strong.
And this love we bear things –
their coarse hide, the blown chaff of their scent –
this love is strong.

Inspiration

Think of those Chinese monks' tales:
years of struggling
in the zendo, then the clink,
while sweeping up, of stone on stone...
It's Emily's wisdom: Truth in Circuit lies.
Or see Grant's *Common Birds And How To Know Them*
(New York: Scribner's, 1901):
'The approach must be by detour,
advantage taken of rock, tree, mound, and brush,
but if without success this way, use artifice,
throw off all stealth's appearance, watchfulness,
look guileless, a loiterer, purposeless,
stroll on (not too directly toward the bird),
avoiding any gaze too steadfast;
or failing still in this, give voice to sundry whistles,
chirp: your quarry may stay on to answer.'
More briefly, try; but stymied, give it up, do something else.
Leave the untrappable thought, go walking,
ideas buzz the air like flies; return to work,
a fox trots by – not Hughes's sharp-stinking thought-fox
but quite real, outside the window,
with cream-dipped tail and red-fire legs doused watery brown;
emerges from the wood's dark margin, stopping all thinking,
and briefly squats (not fox, but vixen), then moves along
and out of sight. 'Enlightenment,' wrote one master,
'is an accident, though certain efforts make you accident-prone.'
The rest slants fox-like, in and out of stones.

The Love of Aged Horses

Because I know tomorrow
his faithful gelding heart will be broken
when the spotted mare is trailered and driven away,
I come today to take him for a gallop on Diaz ridge.

Returning, he will whinny for his love.
Ancient, spavined,
her white parts red with hill-dust,
her red parts whitened with the same, she never answers.

But today, when I turn him loose at the bent gate
with the taste of chewed oat on his tongue
and the saddle-sweat rinsed off with water,
I know he will canter, however tired,
whinnying wildly up the ridge's near side,
and I know he will find her.

He will be filled with the sureness of horses
whose bellies are grain-filled,
whose long-ribbed loneliness
can be scratched into no-longer-lonely.

His long teeth on her withers,
her rough-coated spots will grow damp and wild.
Her long teeth on his withers,
his oiled-teakwood smoothness will grow damp and wild.
Their shadows' chiasmus will fleck and fill with flies,
the eight marks of their fortune stamp and then cancel the earth.
From ear-flick to tail-switch, they stand in one body.
No luck is as boundless as theirs.

Percolation

In this rain that keeps us inside,
the frog,
wisest of creatures,
to whom all things come,
is happy, rasping out of himself
the tuneless anthem of Frog.
Further off and more like ourselves
the cows are raising a huddling protest,
a rag-tag crowd, that can't get its chanting in time.
Now the crickets,
seeming to welcome the early-come twilight,
come in – of all orchestras, the most plaintive.
Still, in this rain soft as fog
that can only be known to be rain by the windows' streaming,
surely all Being at bottom is happy:
soaked to the bone, sopped at the root,
fenny, seeped through, yielding as coffee grounds
yield to their percolation, blushing, completely seduced,
assenting as they give in to the downrushing water,
the murmur of falling, the fluvial, purling wash
of all the ways matter loves matter,
riding its gravity down, into the body,
rising through cell-strands of xylem, leaflet and lung-flower,
back into air.

The Groundfall Pear

It is the one he chooses,
yellow, plump, a little bruised
on one side from falling.
That place he takes first.

A Breakable Spell

I don't know
with what tongue
to answer
this world's constant question –

whether the tongue
of red enamel, or blue,
whether the tongue
of flowing water, or ice,

or the tongue of mountain,
or the split-songed
tongue that embraces first light.

But it keeps asking
and so I continue,
trying *cucumber*, trying *window*,
trying *egret* –

For a moment
she stands with her
elegant legs
black in the water.
Below her, another looks up.

My love,
there is no sound between them.

Then,
inside apples and subways,
in smokestacks,
in blossoming roses,
the heart's machinery starts up again,
hammering and sawing.

The Water Diamonds

Inside perfection, continents could hide;
behind its doors,
the fierce worlds turn unseen –
smooth surfaces, the dragonflies' blue glide,
conceal the swift-fleshed trout, the spotted bream.

But flaked from its long bones by charring heat,
translucent-swimming will
becomes opaque:
unspirits itself edible and sweet,
and will not travel more except the lake

of human understanding, human fate –
Who would have chosen burial
so fearful?
Yet waters roughen, winds uprising late,
and deep fish rise to feed, as if some riddle

drew them upward to be solved.
The slipped scales throw
a night-sky's worth of icy stars
across the catch-pans where they slow-revolve,
like half-dazed planets. Not quite caught, or ours,

not quite anyone's at all....
A herd of water diamonds, perhaps,
stalled
a moment, two,
within their thousand lives' recall.

The Task

It is a simple garment, this slipped-on world.
We wake into it daily – open eyes, braid hair –
a robe unfurled
in rose-silk flowering, then laid bare.

And yes, it is a simple enough task
we've taken on,
though also vast:
from dusk to dawn,

from dawn to dusk, to praise, and not
be blinded by the praising.
To lie like a cat in hot
sun, fur fully blazing,

and dream the mouse;
and to keep too the mouse's patient, waking watch
within the deep rooms of the house,
where the leaf-flocked

sunlight never reaches, but the earth still blooms.

In Yellow Grass

In the yellow grass
each gathers with its own kind –
and the lion-beauty cuts that invisible pen,
the bright wires trampled or leapt.

So, love, it will be with us, both
lion and prey – our mouths so deep in richness
only the wild scent of earth will be left
to tremble, after.

Even the Vanishing Housed

But what if the world's
strict questions were not this
unanswerable yellow, that rampant red,
or the black-hearted, pried-open blue?
If the disciplined welter
were not heady with white-scented bloom?
Would love bend like the tulips then
from its quick-flying carriage?
Would tenderness wring the heart still
of its burdens, leaving only the dark-salted
circles on stone-colored ground?
It is the way humans know –
through the earth, through the things of the earth,
lips stained by what they have tasted,
the sweet sap-run, the tart-rinded fruit.
Leave to dogs and the angels
the music that lies beyond hearing.
Though the infinite palace is infinite, it is precise.

III.

THE OCTOBER PALACE

A Sweetening All Around Me As It Falls

Even generous August,
only a child's scribblings
on thick black paper, in smudgeable chalk –
even the ripening tomatoes, even the roses,
blowsy, loosing their fragrance of black tea.
A winter light held this morning's apples
as they fell, sweet, streaked by one touch
of the careless brush, appling to earth.
The seeds so deep inside they carry that cold.
Is this why some choose solitude, to rise
that small bit further, unencumbered by love of earth,
as the branches, lighter, kite now a little higher
on gold air? But the apples love earth and falling,
lose themselves in it as much as they can at first touch
and then, with time and rain, at last completely:
to be that bone-like One that shines unleafed in winter rain,
all black and glazed with not the pendant gold of
necklaced summer but the ice-color mirroring starlight
when the earth is empty and dark and knows nothing of apples.
Seed-black of the paper, seed-black of the waiting heart –
December's shine, austere and fragile, carves the visible tree.
But today, cut deep in last plums, in yellow pears,
in second flush of roses, in the warmth of an hour, now late,
as drunk on heat as the girl who long ago vanished into green trees,
fold that loneliness, one moment, two, love, back into your arms.

Of the Body

And what of that other net? The one
we willingly give ourselves to, it is that beautiful –
each knot so carefully made, the curved
plate of the sternum tied to the shape of breath,
the perfect hinge of the knee that opens and closes the earth.
The water of the eye very cold, very clear.
And the sturgeon, the golden carp, how they continue to elude us.
Swim straight through and are instantly gone;
though a shadow flickers, remembering.

The Thief

Every fire is stolen.
And so lovers,
after, their arms or thighs touching
lightly, find themselves
even in daylight speaking in whispers.
Not to escape the passionate,
vanquished gods, who, the Greeks told us,
hated our happiness with an inexplicable heat,
but because their tenderness raises
its clear, wild sap in artesian tongues of desire
wedded wholly to jealous time.
For fish, water is endless; for birds, the air.
And our element, endless too.
But who can fin unstoppably in desire,
that lifts and lets go legs, outreaches arms,
quickens and slows even breath? It pins us
to this world we thieve and thieve from, want without pause,
the hunger blossoms first of flower, then snow.
Until the single fragrance spilling and we open
to the dark that comes to take us – embrace
that should be brutal, yet somehow not. No, intimate,
almost a kindness, the quick taking.
And then that too is faithfully stripped from our arms.

Leaving the October Palace

In ancient Japan, to travel
meant always away –
toward the capital, one spoke only of return.
As these falling needles and leaves speak of return,
their long labors of green tired finally into gold,
the desire that remembered them into place
prepared at last to let go.
Though not for want of faithfulness –
all that once followed the sun still follows it now,
as it turns away.
The courtiers assemble their carriages, fold up their robes.
By daybreak, the soundless mountains bow under snow.

Ripeness

Ripeness is
what falls away with ease.
Not only the heavy apple,
the pear,
but also the dried brown strands
of autumn iris from their corm.

To let your body
love this world
that gave itself to your care
in all of its ripeness,
with ease,
and will take itself from you
in equal ripeness and ease,
is also harvest.

And however sharply
you are tested –
this sorrow, that great love –
it too will leave on that clean knife.

The Weighing

The heart's reasons
seen clearly,
even the hardest
will carry
its whip-marks and sadness
and must be forgiven.

As the drought-starved
eland forgives
the drought-starved lion
who finally takes her,
enters willingly then
the life she cannot refuse,
and is lion, is fed,
and does not remember the other.

So few grains of happiness
measured against all the dark
and still the scales balance.

The world asks of us
only the strength we have and we give it.
Then it asks more, and we give it.

Meeting the Light Completely

Even the long-beloved
was once
an unrecognised stranger.

Just so,
the chipped lip
of a blue-glazed cup,
blown field
of a yellow curtain,
might also,
flooding and falling,
ruin your heart.

A table painted with roses.
An empty clothesline.

Each time,
the found world surprises –
that is its nature.

And then
what is said by all lovers:
'What fools we were, not to have seen.'

The Gods Are Not Large

But perhaps
the heart
does not want
to be understood.
Your shadow
falls on its pond
and the small fish
hurry away.
They have
their own lives,
not yours,
which they love.

And if to you
it is anger,
bewilderment,
grief,
to them
it is simply life:
their mouths
open and close,
their gills,
they are fed,
they breathe.

The gods
are not large,
outside us.
They are the fish,
going on
with their own concerns.

The Heart As Origami

Each one has its shape.
For love, two sleeping ducks.
For selfless courage, the war horse.
For fear of death, the daylily's one-day flower.
More and more creased each year, worn paper thin,
and still it longs for them all.
Not one of the lives of this world the heart does not choose.

An Earthly Beauty

Others have described
the metal bull placed over fire,
it singing while the man inside it died.
Which emperor listened, in which country,
doesn't matter, though surely
the thing itself was built by slaves.
An unearthly music, all reports agree.
We – the civilised – hearing this story,
recoil from it in horror: Not us. Not ours.
By why does my heart look back at me,
reproachful? Why does the bull?

Within This Tree

Within this tree
another tree
inhabits the same body;
within this stone
another stone rests,
its many shades of grey
the same,
its identical
surface and weight.
And within my body,
another body,
whose history, waiting,
sings: *there is no other body*,
it sings,
there is no other world.

Empedocles' Physics

In all its parts the deep foul valley trembled so
I thought the universe felt love, which some believe
Has many times returned the world to chaos; here below
And elsewhere in that moment, the ancient cliffsides tumbled.

DANTE, *The Inferno*, CANTO XII

'Aversion carves the self.'
– A Vedic teaching too, though here
it is Empedocles', who wrote
that Hate creates our fractal'd world,
which Love would have a single, formless sphere.
An example: enemy soldiers, late
in 1914, carolled each other across the fields.
Could not, next dawn, take up their former places.
Such is the chaos that affection yields.

When did we cut the long-compounded verbs
into their separate nouns,
the worm's life from the bird's?
Must it be loneliness crowns all things
that live? Packed fat of the sea-lion,
fox blood splashing the brush like early sun –
why give them to our wars to be undone?
But what if in truth Love's perfect One were
Dante's sheered disorder, the known world tumbled?
If the longing and stumble of self were made of sin?
Choose Hate, to stay faceted then
in the many and season-stung minds, the battered salmonskin
peeling its sky's flung rind, the blossoming strife.
Choose the cell's dividing, life into life,
the too-bright stream. Choose beauty loved –
how loved – within division's light.

The Stone of Heaven

Here, where the rivers dredge up
the very stone of Heaven, we name its colors –
muttonfat jade, kingfisher jade, jade of appleskin green.

And here, in the glittering
hues of the Flemish Masters, we sample their wine;
rest in their windows' sun-warmth,
cross with pleasure their scrubbed tile floors.
Everywhere the details leap like fish – bright shards
of water out of water, facet-cut, swift-moving
on the myriad bones.

Any woodthrush shows it – he sings,
not to fill the world, but because he is filled.

But the world does not fill with us,
it spills and spills, whirs with owl-wings,
rises, sets, stuns us with planet-rings, stars.
A carnival tent, a fluttering of banners.

O baker of yeast-scented loaves,
sword dancer,
seamstress, weaver of shattering glass,
O whirler of winds, boat-swallower,
germinant seed,
O seasons that sing in our ears in the shape of O –
we name your colors muttonfat, kingfisher, jade,
we name your colors anthracite, orca, growth-tip of pine,
we name them arpeggio, pond,
we name them flickering helix within the cell, burning coal tunnel,
 blossom of salt,
we name them roof flashing copper, frost-scent at morning,
 smoke-singe of pearl,
from black-flowering to light-flowering we name them,
from barest conception, the almost not thought of, to heaviest
 matter, we name them,
from glacier-lit blue to the gold of iguana we name them,
and naming, begin to see,
and seeing, begin to assemble the plain stones of earth.

from

OF GRAVITY
& ANGELS

(1982–1988)

I.

TO HEAR THE FALLING WORLD

After Work

I stop the car along the pasture edge,
gather up bags of corncobs from the back,
and get out.
Two whistles, one for each,
and familiar sounds draw close in darkness –
cadence of hoof on hardened bottomland,
twinned blowing of air through nostrils curious, flared.
They come, deepened and muscular movements
conjured out of sleep: each small noise and scent
heavy with earth, simple beyond communion,
beyond the stretched out hand from which they calmly
take corncobs, pulling away as I hold
until the mid-points snap.
They are careful of my fingers,
offering that animal-knowledge,
the respect which is due to strangers;
and in the night, their mares' eyes shine, reflecting stars,
the entire, outer light of the world here.

In a Net of Blue and Gold

When the moored boat lifts, for its moment,
out of the water like a small cloud –
this is when I understand.
It floats there, defying the stillness to break,
its white hull doubled on the surface smooth as glass.
A minor miracle, utterly purposeless.
Even the bird on the bow-line takes it in stride,
barely shifting his weight before resuming
whatever musing it is birds do;
and the fish continue their placid, mid-day
truce with the world, suspended a few feet below.
I catch their gleam, the jeweled, reflecting scales,
small dragons guarding common enough treasure.
And wonder how, bound to each other as we are
in a net of blue and gold,
we fail so often, in such ordinary ways.

Invocation

This August night, raccoons,
come to the back door
burnished all summer by salty,
human touch: enter secretly & eat.

Listen, little mask-faced ones,
unstealthy bandits whose tails
are barred with dusk:
listen, gliding green-eyed ones:
I concede you gladly
all this much-handled stuff,
garbage, grain,
the cropped food and cropped heart –
may you gnaw in contentment
through the sleep-hours
on everything left out.

May you find the house
hospitable,
well-used,
stocked with sufficient goods.
I'll settle with your leavings,

as you have settled for mine,
before startling back into darkness
that marks each of us so differently.

To Hear the Falling World

Only if I move my arm a certain way,
it comes back.
Or the way the light bends in the trees
this time of year,
so a scrap of sorrow, like a bird, lights on the heart.
I carry this in my body, seed
in an unswept corner, husk-encowled and seeming safe.
But they guard me, these small pains,
from growing sure
of myself and perhaps forgetting.

Dialogue

A friend says,
'I'm always practising to be an old woman.'
Another answers,
'I see myself young, maybe fourteen.'

But when I lean to that mirror
a blackbird wing rises,
dark, flashing red at the shoulder,

and no woman is there
to pin flowers over the place
where her left breast lifts, falls.

Justice Without Passion

My neighbor's son, learning piano,
moves his fingers through the passages
a single note at a time, each lasting an equal interval,
each of them loud, distinct,
deliberate as a camel's walk through sand.
For him now, all is dispassion, a simple putting in place;
and so, giving equal weight to each mark in his folded-back book,
bending his head towards the difficult task,
he is like a soldier or a saint: blank-faced, and given wholly
to an obedience he does not need to understand.
He is even-handed, I think to myself,
and so, just. But in what we think of as music
there is no justice, nor in the evasive beauty of this boy,
glimpsed through his window across the lawn,
nor in what he will become, years from now, whatever he will become.
For now though, it is the same to him:
right note or wrong, he plays only for playing's sake
through the late afternoon, through stumbling and error,
through children's songs, Brahms, long-rehearsed, steady progressions
as he learns the ancient laws – that human action is judgment,
each note struggling with the rest.
That justice lacking passion fails, betrays.

The Song

The tree, cut down this morning,
is already chainsawed and quartered, stripped
of its branches, transported and stacked.
Not an instant too early, its girl slipped away.
She is singing now, a small figure
glimpsed in the surface of the pond.
As the wood, if taken too quickly, will sing
a little in the stove, still remembering her.

Woman in Red Coat

Some questions cannot be answered.
They become familiar weights in the hand,
round stones pulled from the pocket,
unyielding and cool.
Your fingers travel their surfaces,
lose themselves finally
in the braille of the durable world.
Look out of any window, it's the same –
the yellow leaves, the wintering light.
A truck passes, piled deep in cut wood.
A woman, in a red wool coat,
sees you watching and quickly looks away.

Heat

My mare, when she was in heat,
would travel the fenceline for hours,
wearing the impatience
in her feet into the ground.

Not a stallion for miles, I'd assure her,
give it up.

She'd widen her nostrils,
sieve the wind for news, be moving again,
her underbelly darkening with sweat,
then stop at the gate a moment, wait
to see what I might do.
Oh, I knew
how it was for her, easily
recognised myself in that wide lust:
came to stand in the pasture
just to see it played.
Offered a hand, a bucket of grain,
a minute's distraction from passion
the most I gave.

Then she'd return to what burned her:
the fence, the fence,
so hoping I might see, might let her free.
I'd envy her then,
to be so restlessly sure
of heat, and need, and what it takes
to feed the wanting that we are –

only a gap to open
the width of a mare,
the rest would take care of itself.
Surely, surely I knew that,
who had the power of bucket
and bridle –

she would beseech me, sidle up,
be gone, as life is short.
But desire, desire is long.

Of Gravity & Angels

And suddenly, again,
I want the long road of your thigh
under my hand, your well-travelled thigh,
your salt-slicked & come-slicked thigh,
and I want the taste of you, slaking,
under my tongue (that place of riding desire,
my tongue) and I want
all the unnameable, soft, and yielding places,
belly & neck & the place wings would rise from
if we were angels,
and we are, and I want the rising regions of you
shoulder & cock & tongue & breathing &
suddenness of you
opening
all fontanel, all desire, the whole thing beginning
for the first time again, the first,
until I wonder then how is it
we even know which part we are,
even know the ground that lifts us, raucous,
out of ourselves,
as the rising sound of a summer dawn
when all of it joins in.

I Have No Use for Virgins

I have no use for virgins –
give me the cup
with a chipped lip,
whose handle is glued back on
and whose glaze is dark from use.
Let many men and women
drink from us before
we drink –
I taste their breasts on your breast,
you cover their blaze between my legs.

Tonight the Incalculable Stars

Tonight the incalculable stars
have me thinking of
Catullus and his Lesbia,
who began counting once
and could not stop
until every schoolchild's tongue
pronounced their kisses
interminable,
stumbling through memorised passion
past ancient, jealous crones –
the old arithmetic of love,
got down by heart,
the hard way,
in a foreign tongue, too young.

For What Binds Us

There are names for what binds us:
strong forces, weak forces.
Look around, you can see them:
the skin that forms in a half-empty cup,
nails rusting into the places they join,
joints dovetailed on their own weight.
The way things stay so solidly
wherever they've been set down –
and gravity, scientists say, is weak.

And see how the flesh grows back
across a wound, with a great vehemence,
more strong
than the simple, untested surface before.
There's a name for it on horses,
when it comes back darker and raised: proud flesh,

as all flesh
is proud of its wounds, wears them
as honors given out after battle,
small triumphs pinned to the chest –

And when two people have loved each other
see how it is like a
scar between their bodies,
stronger, darker, and proud;
how the black cord makes of them a single fabric
that nothing can tear or mend.

III.
THE OTHER EARTH

November, Remembering Voltaire

In the evenings
I scrape my fingernails clean,
hunt through old catalogues for new seed,
oil workboots and shears.
This garden is no metaphor –
more a task that swallows you into itself,
earth using, as always, everything it can.
I lend myself to unpromising winter dirt
with leaf-mold and bulb,
plant into the oncoming cold.
Not that I ever thought
the philosopher meant to be taken literally,
but with no invented God overhead,
I conjure a stubborn faith in rotting
that ripens into soil,
in an old corm that rises steadily each spring:
not symbols, but reassurances,
like a mother's voice at bedtime reading a long-familiar book,
the known words barely listened to,
but joining, for all the nights of a life,
each world to the next.

Proteus Entering Water

For him, the world was tangential, to be abandoned,
like the line of his body entering water, turning off
to another angle, another life.
From the trees the shore-birds rose steep-winged and grey,
seeing only the widening rings of fish.
Ripples that intersected where he stood, waist-deep in air,
moving off from him changed.
When the birds entered, their wings so closed it was
another being, oiled and sleek, that pursued.
A short time after, each one reappeared with its prize,
assumed the form, once again, of bird. Not knowing what it had been.
And he, Proteus, had gone –
taking with him all the unmissed, possible realms,
the golden-clawed beings with their many voices,
the lion-colored light.

Evening, Late Fall

It is not this world, then, to blame, with its red
and blue stars, yellow pears, green apples
that carry a scent which can move you to tears.
The others are not unlike this –
the women stand over sinks with their sleeves pushed back,
thin oxen lean into their yokes,
snow falls with impossible lightness in spring.
How do we bear it, then, to guess sometimes
at their lives across the dark?
How they sing as they run cotton towels across porcelain plates?
How they are innocent?

October 20, 1983

On a quiet morning in autumn
I read the ledgers of a war,
as one can any day –
any list biased, dishonest, incomplete,
and still the numbers are kept.
It is true, the papyrus wears thin
after forty centuries.

For the winter garden
roses are pruned and carefully tied,
earth banked up over the roots.
What if after Antigone, the moment of catharsis,
we quarrel in the car going home?
If compassion cannot cure us?
What if we fail?

I look at my hands, my fingernails
still black with chosen labors.
I know that tomorrow I will go out again to mulch,
to bind, to clip, and that no order imposed
is free of guilt.
The line from a Greek chorus:
'Sing Sorrow, Sorrow, but Good win out in the end.'
But who is measuring, what heart would choose this tune?

On Reading Brecht

A child packs snow around a bit of stone
and throws it at his brother.
Each recalls this all his life,
the one who threw, and the one who cried out in surprise.
And whatever there is of love between them includes it.

So too, these words of Brecht's,
who could not forget
what man does to man in the name of art
or country, yet pressed these poems hard,
and threw.

Recalling a Sung Dynasty Landscape

Palest wash of stone-rubbed ink
leaves open the moon: unpainted circle,
how does it raise so much light?
Below, the mountains
lose themselves in dreaming
a single, thatch-roofed hut.
Not that the hut lends meaning
to the mountains or the moon –
it is a place to rest the eye after much traveling,
is all.
And the heart, unscrolled,
is comforted by such small things:
a cup of green tea rescues us, grows deep and large,
a lake.

The Pattern That Connects

Tonight, as you touched my face,
I thought of Gregory's death:
how knowing perhaps that it would please you,
though he had not shaved for weeks,
he asked you to shave him that day.
It is a thing, I realise now,
that neither his wife nor daughter could do;
and I imagine your fingers suddenly less sure,
moving in ways known until then
only from within.
But in your hands' slow remembering
you shaved him as your father had once shaved you,
with large-knuckled, inexpressible joy.
One man can give another so little:
not courage, not time.
The weight of his head for those moments
held in your hand, and then not.
The melody that carries a children's rhyme
through centuries, though the meaning of the words is lost.

Toward the Infinite

You might take it for a given:
how numbers climb
first quickly,
then more slowly toward the infinite,
the way an aging man climbs stairs
first with a hand to the banister,
then pausing between landings,
then not at all.

Or consider the desert fathers,
hunting their God from the bee-hived caves —
how hunger brought him closer,
lessened the distance
between eye and star,
as light became only an absence
of the long familiar dark.

You near it in circles, the way
a dog circles his sleep before lying down:
the ascetics die with their gnosis
concealed among them, sifted, particular sand.
The man moves to a ground-floor flat and brews his tea,
the numbers continue in lengthy approach.
And your eye for a moment settles
on the breast of a strange girl;
you know her then entirely
before she passes out of view.

With Singing and Banners

Demosthenes, a wise man, filled his mouth
with pebbles before speaking,
and a stream which has run ten feet over rocks
is clear, they say, and safe to drink;
yet still we forget what is owed our failures –
blessings, to praise the stumbled on stone.
And forget what we once knew, how to properly greet
old enemies, for whose sake we practise and parry,
become strong:
with singing and banners, with gladness.

Autumn Quince

How sad they are,
the promises we never return to.
They stay in our mouths,
roughen the tongue, lead lives of their own.
Houses built for another to live in;
a succession of milk bottles brought to the door
every morning and taken inside.

And which piece is real?
The music in the composer's ear
or the lapsed one the orchestra plays?
The world is a blurred version of itself –
marred, lovely, and flawed.
It is enough.

Childhood, Horses, Rain

Again rain:
and the world like a fish held
under running water while the knife-blade
smooths the skin of scales.
Its twin eyes open, watching
not-death, not-life.
We shed our wild selves like this,
fearlessly, as water sheds its smoothness under wind,
and the image breaks, the white house, the apple trees,
the horses quivering with late summer flies as they graze,
the hundred wings brushing the lake of their backs.
Or the dog, who, seeing I will not open the door,
lies down at last to sleep: how, in her dream,
she chases down birds and barks softly.
How later the door will open, and she
in all her black and white ecstasy will burst through
to the scent of damp earth, return shaking rain from her
like seeds to the kitchen floor.
It is late and the dishes are finished, put away.
I towel her dry, she offers her feet up easily, as a horse
from long practise eases the farrier's work:
stands patiently at the hiss of hot iron dipped briefly
into a pail, cooled now and shaped to this one
curve of hoof, pared not quite to the quick;
and the swift blows with their stopped-bell ring.
As we learn to stand, for this world.

Lullabye

Lullabye, n.: 1. a song to quiet children or to lull
them to sleep; a cradlesong. 2. music for this.
3. good night or good-by; a farewell
for D.M. (1890-1985)

Always there is desire,
only the shape
of what is desired shifts,
each love giving way to another,
from the first sound
of heartbeat inconceivably, priorly there
and on

into the face that rises like a moon
 beyond world's edge;
into the milk that teaches
 earliest meaning, hunger;
into the tumbling of breast, of belly heat,
 of hands, that encourage the body
 to meaning of its own;
into the close-tucked blankets, nascent trust
 that existence will hold through the night;
into the dangled colors, first temptation,
 that come and go;
 into the song that wanders beyond knowing
 out of lips;
into the climbing bafflement of change;
into the first power,
 to call forth;
into the second power,
 to move;
into the third power,
into the loneliness of self.

And then, desire fully mounted,
the branch full-laden with flower,

white hands of strangers start to summon
an awkward, ground-risen heat,
knowledge takes root in the body daily more sure,
it cries out and cries out again in startled awe –

Until, when the whole music is breaking
full-throated into the ears,
the next desire begins to whisper
into the stateliness of bones, a pull,
into the steadiness of blood, a weight,

and flavors of early apples appear on the tongue,
and feet come to travel the ground more slowly again,
the map of the face grows detailed, a country known;

and the new love comes,
if the heart
will open enough, will let enough go to make room:

love of the structure of things,
 bare branches of trees;
love of the overly large, the poorly made,
 the somehow wrong;
love of the golden net,
 the promises and guile of words;
love of the strength
 that is passing from the legs;
love of the colors
 daily leaving the eyes;
love of the delicacy
 that abandons the wrists;
love of all powers
 that diminish out of the body,
 calling farewell

to the ears that forget to listen,
to the nerve-ends fraying with use,
to the breathing that retrenches into itself,
to the beautiful skin grown tired of dividing the earth

into ours, not ours,
as we tire too, of holding separate,
and love of self that was once so clear
grows suddenly simple, widens,
as a mother's hand smoothing a sheet,
as water that broadens and flattens,
taking the shape of the darkened, still-reflecting world.

from

ALAYA

(1971–1981)

The Stream of It

You might say, a white bird in the snow,
and study it for years.
When the lacquer bucket breaks
water is everywhere.
But water already is everywhere,
and salt: this much I understand
or hope.

The binding shadow, orange,
of an orange peel;
sky painted through the hip of a cow.
What the painters learn is a river,
eye to hand,
the color of earth & mind the same,
and its shadow.
Still, it's an unending struggle
to put it down,
even the best of them
leaving palettes like battlefieds,
strewn with what's past.
An unending struggle just to see what is,
when vision keeps breaking like water
across a stone, a constant rushing,
and light is a salmon
always returning, blindly, to its source.

Those Chinese Poems

Those Chinese poems, the women
endlessly combing their hair,
painting their eyebrows like willow trees,
waiting.

Without the brocade
without the jewel-edged mirror
without the next-morning poem, without hope,
endlessly, this woman
waiting.

Like Salt

held lightly in your hand,
our lives together a continuous chance.

Or frost:
something caught out by morning
in the bright, scoured air,
to shine.

Everything That Is Not You

One gain, one loss,
whatever is said.
And the light streaming in
through Venetian blinds.

As this room could be any room,
these words any words.

The impossible closes around
like a smooth lake
on an early morning swim:
everything that is not you.

December Solstice, '73

The days will be getting longer now.
Outside it is raining and raining.

We spoke so much with the same voice,
how will they tell us apart?
One voice, many mouths,
we are many even alone.

But when the time came,
it darkened & rained through my tongue.

My sleep has the texture of canvas, waiting.
You go out to the streets,
and try to bargain,
driving your life like a nail, deep into time.

I was wrong:
we are foreigners in the same country,
trying to weep.

And learning ourselves
like a hard to decipher book,
we will each come away with separate meanings,
friend.

And

And
yes in the fields you
must wind for me
ropes of wheatstalk
weave me walls
out of husked corn ears
and the shed skins
of a reptile's turnings
in the soil yes & I
will lend you years
of water
fins to bend them
to a circle and to mirrors
of my eyes the sun white
blinding hard behind the shutters
and oh
yes this clapboard house
these rooms cool leaning
each against the other
like a picket fence in spring

[1971]

Jane Hirshfield was born in 1953 in New York City and received her A.B. from Princeton University in 1973. She has lived in northern California since 1974. In 2005 Bloodaxe Books published *Each Happiness Ringed by Lions: Selected Poems*, her first British publication, drawing on five award-winning American collections: *Alaya* (1982), *Of Gravity & Angels* (1988), *The October Palace* (1994), *The Lives of the Heart* (1997) and *Given Sugar, Given Salt* (2001). This was followed by four later collections from Bloodaxe in the UK: *After* (2006), a Poetry Book Society Choice shortlisted for the T.S. Eliot Prize; *Come, Thief* (2012); *The Beauty* (2015); and *Ledger* (2020). In 2008 Bloodaxe and Newcastle University published Jane Hirshfield's Newcastle/Bloodaxe Poetry Lectures, *Hiddenness, Surprise, Uncertainty: Three Generative Energies of Poetry*.

She has also published two collections of essays, *Nine Gates: Entering the Mind of Poetry*, (HarperCollins, 1997) and *Ten Windows: How Great Poems Transform the World* (Knopf, 2015), and has edited and served as co-translator for several acclaimed and much reprinted volumes collecting the work of women poets of the past: *The Ink Dark Moon: Love Poems by Ono no Komachi and Izumi Shikibu, Women of the Ancient Court of Japan* (Scribner's, 1988; Vintage Classics, 1990); *Women in Praise of the Sacred: 43 Centuries of Spiritual Poetry by Women* (HarperCollins, 1994); and *Mirabai: Ecstatic Poems* (Beacon Press, 2004). Her own poetry has been translated into Polish by Czesław Miłosz (among others), who also wrote the introduction for her bestselling Polish Selected Poems, published by Znak in 2002.

She has taught at the University of California, Berkeley, at Stanford University and elsewhere, and has held many residencies. She has had fellowships from the Guggenheim and Rockefeller foundations, the National Endowment for the Arts, and the Academy of American Poets. In 2012 she was elected a Chancellor of the Academy of American Poets, and in 2019 she was inducted into the American Academy of Arts and Sciences.